Dachshunds

The Owner's Guide from Puppy to Old Age

Choosing, Caring for, Grooming, Health, Training
and Understanding Your Standard or Miniature
Dachshund Dog

By Alex Seymour

Copyright and Trademarks

This publication is Copyright © 2016 by CWP Publishing.

ISBN: 978-1-910677-05-6

Disclaimer and Legal Notice

This book has been written to provide useful information on the Dachshund. It should not be used to diagnose or treat any medical condition. For diagnosis or treatment of any animal medical condition consult a qualified veterinarian. The author and publishers are not responsible or liable for any specific health or allergy conditions that may require medical supervision and are not liable for any damages or negative consequences from any treatment, action, application, or preparation, to any person reading or following the information in this book. References are provided for informational purposes only and do not constitute endorsement of any websites or other sources mentioned. We have no control over the nature, content and availability of the websites listed.

While every attempt has been made to verify the information shared in this book, neither the author nor the affiliates assume any responsibility for errors, omissions or contrary interpretation of the subject matter herein. Any perceived slights to any specific person(s) or organization(s) are purely unintentional. The information in this book is not intended to serve as legal advice.

Foreword

Congratulations on purchasing this book. You've made a wise choice as many of the world's top breeders have been involved in contributing to this book, and once you've reached the end, you will have all the information you need to make a well-informed decision whether or not the Dachshund is the breed for you.

As an expert trainer and professional dog whisperer, I will teach you the human side of the equation, so you can learn how to think more like your Dachshund and eliminate behavioral problems.

While this is an exceptional breed with unique and endearing qualities, it is imperative that you understand the things that make these dogs different and what they will need from you in care and companionship before you proceed. That is the purpose of this book. No matter how cute Dachshunds are, they must only go to the right people, to owners who can understand and take responsibility for the breed's emotional as well as physical needs.

Dachshunds are fantastic companions, affectionate, intelligent, brave to a fault, and truly comical. However, they also can be willful and headstrong. The breed's elongated physical form also can make them prone to a range of spinal issues. Fortunately, most back problems can be avoided by buying your dog from a healthy bloodline, keeping him fit and trim and using common sense with physical activities.

If you learn everything you can about Dachshunds, take a realistic look at your life and home, and decide this is the breed for you, you will never regret the decision. But being responsible in truly considering the ramifications of any pet ownership is a huge part of being a good owner. If you don't do the hard thinking first, before the fun starts, the dog is the one who will face the consequences of your bad choice, but, choose wisely and well, taking into consideration your needs and those of the Dachshund, and you will have one of the best canine companions you could ever hope to meet.

FREE BONUS

DACHSHUND BREEDER INTERVIEWS

As a **special thank you** for buying this book we would like to give you even more value by **giving you free access** to some exclusive bonus interviews with expert Dachshund breeders.

This enables you to stay in touch after you have read the book and get even more useful and entertaining Dachshund advice and tips.

GET THE FREE BONUS INTERVIEWS...

Go to this page on our website to download your free gift:

http://www.dogexperts.info/dachshund/gift

Acknowledgments

In writing this book, I also sought tips, advice, photos, and opinions from many experts of the Dachshund breed. In particular, I wish to thank the following wonderful breeders, organizations, owners, and vets for their outstanding help and contribution:

United States and Canada Contributors

Vicki Spencer of Lorindol Standard Smooths and secretary of the Dachshund Club of America
Email: lorindol@roadrunner.com

Lorraine and Dave Simmons of Stardox Dachshunds
Email: Stardox2@yahoo.com

Acknowledgments

Andra O'Connell of Amtekel Longhair Dachshunds and former Dachshund Club of America Secretary from 1999-2006
http://www.amtekel.com/

Maggie Peat of Pramada Kennels
http://www.pramadakennels.com/

Tom Sikora of Koradox Dachshunds
http://koradox.com/

Karen Scheiner of Harlequin Dachsunds
http://www.harlequindachshunds.com/

Sheila DeLashmutt of ZaDox Dachshunds
http://www.zadoxdachshunds.com

Carol "Jeani" McKenney of Tarabon Dachshunds
Email: mctarabon@aol.com

Sheila Paske of Storybook Dachshunds
http://www.storybookdachshunds.com/

Amanda Hodges of Teckelwood Dachshunds
http://www.teckelwood.com

Anne Schmidt of Stardust Dachshunds
http://www.stardustdachshunds.com/

Connie & Gary Fisher of Beldachs Between the Hills
http://www.beldachs.com

Lucy Granowicz of Von Links Dachshunds
http://www.vonlinksdachshunds.com

Kelly Denise Bensabat of Splendor Farms
http://www.splendorfarms.com

Cyndi Branch of Willow Springs Dachshunds
http://www.willowspringsdachshunds.com/

Acknowledgments

Dianne Graham of Diagram Dachshunds
Email: diagramdachshunds@gmail.com

Lori Darling of Red Oak Dachshunds
http://www.redoakdachshunds.com/

Audrey Paul of Small Wonders Kennels
http://www.smallwonderskennel.com

Cyndy Senff of Dynadaux Miniatures
http://www.dynadaux.com

Shirley Ray of Raydachs
http://www.raydachs.com

Emma Jean Stephenson of EJ's Miniature Dachshunds
http://www.ejsdachshunds.net

Jerry Cerasini of Brownwood Farms
http://brownwoodfarm.com/

Debby Krieg of Daybreak Wires
http://www.daybreakwires.com

Lynn Cope of Jeric's Kennels
http://www.jerics-dachshunds.com/

Midge Martin of Full Circle Dachshunds
Email: kaihorn@att.net

Helen 'Dee Dee' Clarke of Deedachs Kennel
http://www.deedachs.com/

Joyce Wilson of Re:Joyce Dachshunds
http://www.rejoycewiredachshunds.com/

Lois and Ralph Baker of Louie's Dachshunds
http://www.louiesdachshunds.com/

Travis Wright of RoundAbout Dachshunds
http://www.roundaboutkennel.com/

Catherine Johnson of Peachtree Kennel
http://www.peachtreedachshunds.com/

United Kingdom Contributors

Ian Seath, Chairman of the UK Dachshund Breed Council
http://dachshundbreedcouncil.org.uk/

Mandy Dance of Emem Dachshunds
http://www.ememdachshunds.co.uk

Debbie Clarke of Tekalhaus Dachshunds
http://www.tekalhausdachshunds.com

Susan Holt of Waldmeister Dachshunds
http://www.waldmeisterdachshunds.co.uk/

Nora and Paul Price of Samlane Dachshunds
http://www.samlanedachshunds.co.uk/

Pat Endersby of Mowbray Dachshunds
http://www.mowbraydachshunds.co.uk

Sue Ergis of Siouxline Dachshunds
http://www.siouxline.co.uk/

Australia Contributors

Judy Poulton of Laurieton Dachshunds
http://www.laurietondachshunds.com/

Avril Osborne of Dachshund Dawgz
http://www.dachshunddawgz.com/

Table of Contents

Table of Contents

Table of Contents

Table of Contents

Table of Contents

Table of Contents

Chapter 1 – Meet the Dachshund

From their origin as hunting dogs to their popular acceptance as pets in the early 1900s, the intelligent, tenacious, and ridiculously brave Dachshund is one of the most popular of all companion breeds. Athletic, entertaining, and packed with attitude, this is a big dog in a little, elongated package.

Photo Credit: Andra O'Connell of Amtekel Longhair Dachshunds

The distinctive body conformation and hound-like head is testament to the Dachshund's original purpose. Dachshund is a German word literally translating into English as "badger dog." First mentioned in the 1500s, "Dachshunds" were dogs with the courage to go to ground with the vicious and ill-tempered badgers.

Hunters didn't care about having purebred dogs for such a purpose. They only wanted dogs that would get the job done. They did, however, selectively breed their top performers and over time, the genesis of a purebred "badger dog" with ideal characteristics emerged.

These included the keen tracking senses of a hound, short legs and long bodies to enter the badger's den, and the bravery to face the cornered creature head on. The Dachshund is classified in the hound group or scent hound group in the United States and Great Britain, and as a dwarf breed are more susceptible to back disease than most other breeds, nevertheless they are generally recognized as a healthy breed. You just need to be sensible and don't allow them to jump on and off beds or furniture.

Known in Germany today as the Dachshund, Dachsel, Dackel, and Teckel, and lovingly in the United States as a Doxie, hot dog, Weiner dog, or sausage dog, this is a unique breed with a fascinating and often challenging personality.

This book covers the two main sizes — **standards** and **miniatures**. Even then, each size comes in **three different** coat types, making six possibilities to choose from — as if it wasn't hard enough already! Don't worry — we are here to guide you with expert breeder advice along the way so you really get to know the Dachshund inside out.

Over **40 experienced breeders** from all over the world have kindly given their time to answer questions and give their expert advice. You are about to benefit from literally hundreds of years experience of breeding and living with Dachshunds.

Breeder **Vicki Spencer of Lorindol Standard Smooths** is also **secretary of the Dachshund Club of America**, and she tells us why she chose this breed above all others: "I began actively showing Golden Retrievers in obedience and conformation in 1970. In 1994 I acquired a Dachshund puppy who became American Dual Champion, Canadian Champion, International Champion Cherevee Bad News Bear VC (Versatility Certificate) JE (Junior Earth Dog) CD (Companion Dog) titling in conformation, field trials, obedience and earthdog. Needless to say I was hooked.

"Why a Dachshund (especially since they are polar opposites from a Golden Retriever)? I love their intelligence, independence and tenacity. Even though they love their people to the nth degree and are extremely eager to please, they have a stubbornness that will keep you on your toes. Being tremendously intelligent, they have no problem questioning your orders if they feel you are being unreasonable. They are free thinkers who can and will figure out solutions to problems on their own. Their stubbornness will keep them on a problem until they do figure out a solution.

"Author Steven Rowley hit it right on the head in his book, 'Lilly and the Octopus' when he said, 'By then I had all but given up trying to out-stubborn a Dachshund, an exercise in futility if there ever was one.'

"They love their people unconditionally, but can spot a phony in a heartbeat. Don't bother about trying to trick a Dachshund. They will have you figured out in no time.

"A Dachshund is a hunting dog and should be able to work tirelessly in the field all day. They are fearless to the point of rashness and possess an amazing ability to follow a track. They are friendly and outgoing dogs, but will stand their ground to protect those who are fortunate to be loved by one. They love to play, but also are content to lay quietly by their owner's side.

"Fearless, friendly, devoted and intelligent – I think that says it all."

Want more reasons to choose a Dachshund?

Jerry Cerasini of Brownwood Farms says, "The reason I chose Dachshunds and still love and appreciate them every day is because I have never had a more loyal companion animal. My dogs love me to an extent I have never known from any other breed I have ever owned. This is paired with their ability to think for themselves. If I tell them to do something, they, unlike other breeds, look at me and decide if this is something they would like to do. If not I get a look that says, I don't think so, not today anyway. I love this attitude. I am sure it's not for everyone, but I totally love this combination."

The History of the Dachshund

Historical illustrations from the 15th-17th century show dogs much like Dachshunds used for various hunting purposes. The animals are described as having tracking abilities similar to hounds, but with a physical size and temperament more akin to terriers.

As the Dachshund developed as a distinct breed in Germany, their hunting skills expanded beyond their primary function as badger dogs. Dachshunds are excellent trackers, and are still used today to locate wounded deer. Packs of Dachshunds have been used to hunt wild boar, to go after fox and rabbit, and even to work as retrievers of waterfowl.

It is unclear exactly which breeds were used to cultivate the Dachshund as we know him today. A smaller Pointer, the Braque or

Bracke, a progenitor of many modern hunting dogs, is part of the mix, as is the smooth-coated German Pinscher, popular for its vermin-killing skill.

Photo Credit: Cyndi Branch of Willow Springs Dachshunds.

The strongest ties, however, are to the now-extinct "turnspit" dog, a breed used throughout Europe to walk on a treadmill to power revolving roasting spits. Descriptions of turnspit dogs from the mid-1700s characterize them as animals with stubby legs and extended bodies. Their coats could be short or long, grizzled or spotted, and they had the unusual feature of crooked front legs.

Dachshund paintings from the 19th century show the same type of front legs, leading some canine historians to theorize that the only difference in a "turnspit" dog and a "Dachshund" was the owner and the animal's purpose. Peasants owned turnspit dogs and noblemen owned Dachshunds.

Two different sizes of Dachshund developed according to function. Those (standard size) dogs weighing in a range of 30-35 lbs. / 13.61-15.88 kg were used to hunt badgers and wild boar, while (miniature size) dogs of 16-22 lbs. / 7.26-9.98 kg proved better suited for fox and hare.

Dachshunds were first imported into America in 1885, and the **Dachshund Club of America** was founded in 1895. The breed was added to the American Kennel Club field trials in 1935.

In the United Kingdom, the Dachshund was used as a working dog and was even part of royal kennels. We know the **UK Dachshund Club** was formed in 1881, so there is a long history to this wonderful dog.

These days of course the Dachshund is best known as a pet rather than working dog (although they are still used to track deer and other animals), but you can give your dog the opportunity to do what comes naturally by competing in Dachshund Field Trials and Earthdog events.

In America, the first Dachshund field trial was held in 1935 in Lamington, New Jersey with a total of 13 entries. Since then field trials have become wildly popular with many trials seeing 80 to 100 entries competing each day. The popularity of field trials is due largely to the Dachshund's enthusiasm for hunting and owners enjoying watching their dogs do what they do best.

Famous Dachshund Owners

Dachshunds have certainly found their way into the company of the rich and famous and have, undoubtedly, made their opinions known to everyone. Famous Dachshund owners include:

- James Dean
- Marlon Brando
- John Wayne
- Clint Eastwood
- Doris Day
- Rita Hayworth
- Joan Crawford
- Elizabeth Taylor

- Napoleon
- Gandhi
- E.B. White
- William Faulkner
- Teddy Roosevelt
- John F. Kennedy
- David Hockney
- Frida Kahlo
- Andy Warhol
- Picasso
- George Stephanopoulos (ABC News)
- Sharon Stone
- Kelsey Grammar
- Thom Browne (fashion designer) and his partner Andrew Bolton (curator of historical fashion at MOMA)
- Jim Palmer — baseball hall of fame pitcher

That's the history; now what can you expect of the modern day Dachshund? **Lucy Granowicz of Von Links Dachshunds** says, "Dachshunds are a very loyal breed that love people and thrive on attention. They are very smart and know just how to manipulate their owners. They also can be very funny in the things that they do. All three coats have their own distinct personalities."

What Does the Dachshund Look Like?

In its modern form, the Dachshund is a muscular dog with a long body. He stands on short but sturdy legs with over-sized, paddle-shaped front paws that are ideal for digging.

The deep chest and tubular body accommodates a larger-than-average set of lungs. This allows the breed to hunt underground more efficiently and gives them a deep, sonorous bark, which they are able to sustain for extended periods.

Even with a recognized reputation for developing back problems, this is a strong and hardy breed with an average lifespan of 15 years.

One key advantage is that Dachshunds do not generally smell. A strong odour is not normal and may indicate a skin problem.

Kelly Denise Bensabat of Splendor Farms says: "The life expectancy of a Dachshund, miniature or standard, is usually 12-18 years of age, depending on quality of life, i.e. nutrition, wellness (dental, vaccination/heartworm) and genetics. Personally, I have owned, bred, and buried Dachshunds living to be 19 years of age and have two clients who have owned Dachshunds that lived to be 20!"

They Come in Three Sizes

There are three sizes of Dachshund: standard, miniature, and kaninchen ("rabbit" in German). The latter is not recognized in either the United States or the UK, but is accepted by the World Canine Federation, which has member clubs in 83 countries. Typical weight for the kaninchen is 8-11 lbs. / 3.6-5 kg, and they must have a chest circumference of 30cm or under at 15 months.

Dogs that fall between the standard and miniature are called "tweenies" and are increasingly favored as family dogs. These Dachshunds are often pet-quality animals from reputable breeders and are perfect in every other way except size and are thus not suitable for breeding programs or showing.

Standards

This is the largest sized Dachshund with a typical height of 8-9 inches (20-23 cm). A mature standard Dachshund weighs approximately 16-32 lbs. / 7.3-15 kg (USA breed standard).

Standards come in comes in three different coat varieties — shorthaired (smooth), longhaired, and wirehaired (as explained further in this chapter).

Miniatures

Miniatures are of course smaller in size when compared to

standards. They must weigh a maximum of 11 lbs. / 4.98 kg (this is when they are 1 year old), and are usually 5-6 inches (13-15 cm) in height (USA breed standard).

Miniatures also come in the three different coat varieties — short-haired (smooth), long-haired, and wire-haired.

Note that compared to standards, as a general rule of thumb many minis don't like the rain — a lot of them prefer to be inside. Some breeders also believe they bark a LOT more, have a different temperament (not all, but many), and have more health issues such as with their teeth.

If you are now wondering which of the two sizes to choose, here is some help from **Dianne Graham of Diagram Dachshunds**: "I think size is a matter of where you live and your own personal taste. Some people like to cuddle with a lap full of miniatures while other folks like a standard to lay beside them when sitting on the couch.

"Smaller dogs can live in apartments with walks in local parks. Bigger dogs need a bit more room, but can be managed in smaller spaces, also.

"For older folks, smaller dogs may be the way to go. They are easier to pick up and transport than their bigger relatives.

"Families with young children may do better with standards. The bigger dogs are sturdier than miniatures and make great companions for kids.

"By the way, I have standard smooths and mini wires and can't imagine life without either!"

The Three Distinctly Different Coat Types

Three coat types are present in Dachshunds: shorthair or smooth, longhair, and wirehair. The smooth and longhair varieties have been present since the 16th century. The wirehaired coat with a soft undercoat appeared around 1797. Longhaired Dachshunds have silky hair with short "feathers" on the legs and ears.

Short/Smooth-haired – Dense, short, smooth, and shiny requiring little maintenance.

Sue Ergis of Siouxline Dachshunds has chosen to concentrate on the miniature smooth-haired Dachshund (see her photo) because: "In 1993 after having spent the previous 20 years showing and breeding Basset Hounds I wanted a smaller hound breed to complement the Bassets, a breed that was game and hardy like the

Bassets but a lot smaller. I first had a Standard Dachshund but as they are not much smaller than a Basset, I decided to go smaller with the Miniature. Basset Hounds have a smooth coat and as I'd tried a Dachshund with a long coat I wanted to go back to smooth coats again. Much easier to look after, no matting, no smell.

"I found it quite a challenge breeding the Miniature Smooths for the show ring. Breeding correct construction and soundness within the Kennel Club breed standard for Dachshunds, there is no coat to hide any faults so 'what you see is what you get' … the idea being that they have to be as perfect as possible! I was lucky enough to start off with some really good bloodlines, the result being that I have bred and owned 14 champion Min. Smooth Dachshunds. All this has made it great fun and such a lovely breed to live with."

Sheila Paske of Storybook Dachshunds explains why she has chosen to concentrate on the standard smooth-haired Dachshund: "Simply because I personally like a larger dog. Both in the field and underground, both sizes excel, and in my experience the hunting skills of the two sizes are the same. Many people like a dog which can be carried, but I simply want 'more' dog.

"As for what a new owner can expect — This is an independent, energetic, loyal and friendly breed. They make amazing family companions and are wonderful with children. In my experience, once you have owned a Dachshund, you'll never want to be without one — at least one, as they do very well in a home with more than one. Housebreaking is a matter of consistency and perseverance, but is not an insurmountable task."

Longhaired – Soft and straight with feathering on underparts, ears, behind legs and tail where it forms a flag. Regular grooming is necessary.

Debbie Clarke of Tekalhaus Dachshunds has chosen to concentrate on standard longhaired Dachshunds (see Debbie's photo) because "They have fabulous temperaments, easy to live with, no health issues, are the best of the varieties for families and mix very well with other breeds (we had Rottweilers with them and now have a rescue crossbreed from Mauritius)."

Wirehaired – A short, harsh coat with a dense undercoat covers the body. There is a beard on the chin, eyebrows are bushy but hair on the ears is almost smooth. They don't molt and a wire coat will typically need stripping (not clipping) twice a year, which is explained in the chapter on grooming.

Shirley Ray of Raydachs: "I choose to breed only 1 size (standard) and 1 coat variety (wire) and have been for almost 25 years. I personally believe for a person to truly put everything you can into it is to breed only 1 coat and 1 size. Researching pedigrees and knowing all the dogs and their traits in that pedigree is very important. I also do not cross coats. Some people will breed a wire to a smooth thinking they will get better coats. This is not necessarily so. Many of the smooths have been crossed with longs in the past. The longhair gene can remain in the pedigrees for many many generations. So, when you cross a wire and smooth you can get a very fuzzy cotton type coat. This cannot be stripped out. Looks like a poodle type coat. As the coat is clippered it can become very light, almost white in color. They also can have the longhair ear set. So, I don't believe in crossing coats."

Cyndi Branch of Willow Springs Dachshunds focuses on the miniature wirehaired (see Cyndi's photo below) as a result of: "When my husband and I met our first wirehaired Dachshund in Austria 25 years ago we were instantly captivated — it was love at first sight. She was friendly, outgoing and playful. We find the wires to be affectionate, determined and very good natured. Combine that with their beards and bushy eyebrows and you will smile every time you look at them. We were drawn to the miniature size because we like to be able to take our dogs with us everywhere we go."

Which to Choose?

There is no such thing as the best type as each of the six varieties has its own fans and there is undoubtedly a Dachshund to suit everyone's preference of coat, color, and size. You may however be wondering which is the most popular combination out of the six.

In the United States, we can't say for sure because the American Kennel Club does not divide Dachshunds by size, so there is no record of which size has the most registrations. Vicki Spencer of the Dachshund Club of America says, "In terms of coats, for years it has been smooth coats, followed by longs and finally wires, but wires and longs are certainly becoming more popular. In terms of size, I would guess the miniature smooths because as Breeder Referral for DCA, I get far more calls looking for miniature smooths than any of the other size/variety combination."

In the United Kingdom, the Kennel Club does have the numbers and they show the mini-smooths way out in front in terms of numbers being registered.

Type	2015 Registrations
Miniature Smooths	3450
Miniature Long-Haired	844
Miniature Wire-Haired	717
Standard Wire-Haired	462
Standard Long-Haired	163
Standard Smooths	157

Most Popular Colors

There are seven colors and five patterns found in Dachshunds. For instance, one of the most popular is the black-and-tan marking similar to the coat of a Rottweiler. It is possible for Dachshunds with different coat colors and patterns to be born into the same litter depending on the genetics of the parents.

According to the American Kennel Club, the following is a complete listing of possible Dachshund colors and markings.

- black (considered non-standard color)
- black and cream
- black and tan
- blue and cream
- chocolate (solid chocolate considered non-standard color)
- chocolate and cream
- chocolate and tan
- cream
- fawn
- fawn and cream
- fawn and tan
- red
- wheaten
- wild boar

Markings

- brindle
- dapple
- sable
- brindle piebald
- double dapple
- piebald

You should be very careful of any breeders offering "rare colors" such as double dapple. Breeding dapple to dapple is not something responsible breeders do. Offspring of two dapples may be blind, may lack eyes, or may be deaf. If they appear normal, they will still carry the genes that may cause this to occur.

The dominant color for the breed is red, followed by the black and tan combination. Reds can range from a light copper color to deep rust, with dark hairs present on the back, face, and edge of the ears.

Amanda Hodges of Teckelwood says: "The most popular color for a Dachshund depends on which size and which variety. I think it would be reasonably accurate to say red is the most popular color for standard longhairs. I've found people usually want a black and tan in miniature smooth Dachshunds – unless they only want a red or some pattern. I see more wild boars in wirehairs at the show ring. I've found many people want a red or a cream in miniature

longhairs – but, again, if they want a black and tan or one of the patterns, they won't consider anything else."

Photo Credit: Kelly Denise Bensabat of Splendor Farms with an English Shaded cream and a Pale EE Cream

Eye Color

Eyes are typically a dark brown color. Dachshunds with light colored coats have eyes that are light brown, amber, or green. Dapple Dachshunds may have eyes of two different colors. It is also possible for blue or partially blue eyes to be present in the breed, but this is considered an undesirable trait.

The Dachshund Puppy

Bringing a new puppy home is fun, even if the memories you're making include epic, puppy-generated messes! Young Dachshunds are a huge responsibility no matter how much you love them, and they take a lot of work. Dachshund pups are **curious** and they often will have short, chaotic bursts of energy for around 10 minutes until they calm down again!

The first few weeks with any dog **is an important phase** that shapes the animal's adult behavior and temperament. Every new pet owner hopes to have a well-mannered, obedient, and happy companion.

Puppy proofing, house training, grooming, and feeding aren't the sole requirements. Critical socialization must also occur, including crate training. These measures prevent problem behaviors like whining, biting, or jumping.

To achieve these goals, **you must understand** the breed with which you're working. You will need to train him to understand that you are above him in the pecking order and teach him some basic house rules, and you will be rewarded with a companion for life.

If you don't have the time to spend working with your Dachshund in the areas that will make him a desirable companion, ask yourself if this is really the time in your life to have a pet.

Also, bear in mind that you are also your Dachshund's companion. This is not a one-sided relationship. What is your work schedule? Do you have to travel often and for extended periods? Only purchase a Dachshund if you have time to spend with him.

Initially you will need to devote several hours a day to your new puppy. You have to housetrain and feed him every day, giving him your attention and starting to slowly introduce the house rules as well as take care of his general health and welfare. Remember too that treating Dachshunds like babies is something many owners succumb to and this is not at all good for them.

Certainly for the first few days (ideally two weeks) one of your family **should be around** at all times of the day to help him settle and to start bonding with him. The last thing you should do is buy a puppy and leave him alone in the house after just a day or two. Left alone all day, they will feel isolated, bored, and sad, and this leads to behavioral problems.

As well as time, there is a financial cost, not just the initial cost of your puppy. You also have to be prepared to spend money on regular healthcare, as well as potential emergency money in vet's bills in the case of illness as well as equipment such as crates, bedding, and toys.

DID YOU KNOW? Research shows many dogs have intelligence and understanding levels similar to a two-year-old child. They can understand around 150 words and can solve problems as well as devise tricks to play on people and other animals.

Personality and Temperament

So what defines your Dachshund's character? One factor is his **temperament**, which is an inherited trait, and another factor is the **environment** in which your Dachshund grows up. In a dog's life, the first few months are deemed really important. When the time comes that he becomes separated from the litter, his reactions and responses to the world around him are a reflection of how he has learned the essence of socialization.

There is no denying the **benefits** that your Dachshund gets from being introduced early to other dogs and humans along with different noises and smells. When a dog learns how to feel comfortable in whatever type of surrounding he is in, feelings of fear and anxiety can be eliminated. Otherwise these feelings can cause a dog to display undesirable behavior such as aggression.

Although all dogs are individuals, Dachshunds have well-known personality traits you should understand before you bring one of these **single-minded little dogs** into your home. Dachshunds are incredibly strong willed. It will take effort on your part to assume your proper role as leader of the pack.

By breeding, Dachshunds are **hunters and trackers**. They are exceptionally talented at detecting and following scents, ignoring all commands to the contrary. Always keep your Dachshund on a leash in an open area!

This ability does, however, translate to outstanding performances chasing and finding balls and other toys and a great affinity for participation in field trials and agility competitions.

Dachshunds can also be inveterate diggers. They will go under fences, uproot flowerbeds, and rip up carpet in their conviction that something is down there they *must* uncover. Always keep Dachshunds in a fenced area with footing buried at least 12 inches / 30.48 cm. Dachshunds enjoy having their own sandbox where they are allowed to dig to their heart's content.

Although Dachshunds can suffer from **back problems**, these are truly athletic dogs. They like to move and exercise. Most "bad" behavior is actually an expression of abject boredom. If you are a sedentary person, this may not be the breed for you. You should exercise caution with allowing Dachshunds to play in such a way that they jump excessively, shake their necks, or round sharp corners suddenly. All such activities can lead to spinal ailments.

Anne Schmidt of Stardust Dachshunds: "They really should have a fenced area to run, putting them on a tie outdoors is not safe (they tangle due to their short legs) and can lead to frustration. Stairs do not hurt standard sized Dachshunds, it helps build their core muscles which makes their backs stronger. What they should NOT do is jump off high furniture (your bed) and run circles indoors. Running outdoors on grass is not a problem!!"

Vicki Spencer of Lorindol Standard Smooths adds: "Dachshunds are not foo-foo dogs, they are active hunters who when bred correctly can run, climb and play with no qualms. IF they are bred correctly (ribbing twice as long as the loin to support the back) and IF they are kept at a correct weight a Dachshund should not experience back problems. My dogs hunt, climb, jump and run and I have been fortunate to not have experienced a back problem in the almost 30 years I have owned Dachshunds."

Make no mistake: regardless of any other personality traits, Dachshunds see themselves as the center of the universe. They like to have the spotlight and are quite good at taking it for themselves. They want and need your attention and will get it, one way or another – even if it means they're going to get yelled at.

Lorraine Simmons of Stardox Dachshunds adds: "In the thirty-six years I have had Dachshunds I have found that the temperament or personality can be different in all three coats as well as the sizes. For example, The Long Hair Dachshunds have a softer sweet personality whereas the Wire Hair can have a Terrier type personality. The Smooth Hair Dachshunds are in the middle of the other two. They can be sweet and mushy as well as independent. In the smooths the males tend to adore you more than the females.

Females tend to be more independent.

"The minis tend to have a mini dog type personality which can be busier and more active than standards. Standard Dachshunds tend to have more of a larger dog personality. Dachshunds are scent hounds. They can be stubborn. They need to learn you are the pack leader."

Andra O'Connell of Amtekel, a former (1999-2006) Dachshund Club of America Secretary, says that the temperament of the Dachshund varies slightly between the coats: "The longhair (my variety) is typically the easy going, laid back variety probably from the Spaniel influence that produced the long hair. The wire coats are thought to be the 'clowns' and have a bit more terrier influence while the smooth are perhaps somewhere between the previous two. The Dachshund is small in stature and big on personality. They are a big dog in a small body (no one has informed them that they are indeed a small dog!). They were bred for the tenacity of the hunt and there should be no shyness in this breed. They should also not be aggressive or mean. The Dachshund should be a great family dog who can hunt all day and be peaceful on the couch or with children at night."

Getting Along With Other Pets

Dachshunds are typically good with other pets in the family, but may develop jealousies and grudges depending on the dynamics of

the household.

Even if you can't engineer a total peace agreement with the resident feline, détente is an option. Don't force the animals to interact or to spend time together. When the puppy first arrives, put the little dog in its crate and allow the cat to check out the new member of the family. Expect caution and vocal disapproval.

Supervise all interactions and do this in neutral territory. Reinforce good behavior with treats and praise. Don't over-react to aggression or "trash talking." At this stage, the puppy is likely the one in need of rescuing from potential sharp-clawed swipes.

Separate the animals with a firm "no" and try again later. Understand this can go on for several weeks until your pets reach some form of agreement whose terms only they will comprehend.

As for other kinds of animals, exercise reasonable caution and use your judgment. For instance, never let any dog play with a rabbit. Remember, by breeding, Dachshunds are hunting dogs.

Midge Martin of Full Circle Dachshunds says: "I have had cats and dogs together for many years. Introducing a new animal into the mix is always a challenge. Bringing in a cat, one must be prepared for fireworks, but hope that none occur. The first consideration is that the cat has to have an escape hatch. Dogs will chase...it's their nature, so you have to be sure that the cat cannot be cornered anywhere. Most cats have claws, so you must be sure to supervise any early interaction.

"Yes, Dachshunds are hunters, but they learn about the comforts of the couch early. If you have more than one dog, try to introduce each one to a new cat or dog individually. Pack mentality can take over if there are numbers, so careful introductions and supervision are key.

"The same rules apply for bringing in a new puppy or older dog. Introduce individually...usually the new one on a leash with the new family. Gradually allow for sniffing and play until the newcomer and longer residents are comfortable with each other."

Are Dachshunds Good With Children?

Dachshunds do make for a **good family pet**, especially as they are so loyal to their owners, although they do best around children when they are raised with them as a puppy.

Adult dogs that have not been exposed to babies may find their crying and sudden movements unsettling. Until the dog is socialized with the baby and understands, it may be best to keep them separated.

Even if you do not have children, it's advisable to expose your dog to children during puppyhood to prepare the animal to behave correctly during any future encounters. Supervise these meetings to ensure the children are kind and respectful with the puppy, but do not isolate the dog. Being good around children is a critical part of any well-behaved dog's repertoire of manners.

If you do have children, teach them to interact with all animals in a gentle and proper way. **Regardless, you should not** leave a young child unsupervised with a dog regardless of breed or perceived nature. If a child hurts the dog by pulling its ears or tail or even biting the creature, don't blame the dog for reacting. Ideally I would suggest waiting until your children are 4-5 years of age, when they are old enough to understand the

Dachshund's disposition and to respect his boundaries. With very young children, I guess instead of the miniature size I'd consider perhaps the more sturdier standard sized Dachshund.

Photo Credit: Audrey Paul of Small Wonders Kennels

Travis Wright of RoundAbout Dachshunds says: "We have twin three year-old daughters and a teenage son, so are very familiar with the challenges of balancing the needs of children and mini wires. Fortunately, we've found that with close supervision and training, doxies and even young children can be good friends. Socialization, for both puppies and children, is critical. We start early — introducing the puppies to the kids, and the kids to the puppies. We don't tolerate rough or aggressive play from either, and explain to our girls that dogs like 'nice touches.' When puppies get too rough with the girls or mouth their fingers when teething, we respond with a firm, 'No!' Soon enough, all parties seem to get the point. Now, the girls are experts at lead-training our RoundAbout babies!

"For prospective owners with young children, I'd encourage them to select a puppy from a breeder who has socialized her/his dogs with children of all ages. This helps to make sure the puppy is confident enough around children to tolerate their odd sounds and movements. Likewise, temperament is key — a shy, reserved, or anxious puppy should never be considered for a home with children. When inviting a puppy to live in a home with children, it is important to have a crate or other safe space for the puppy to retreat to when the kids become too much! And, young children and dogs should never be left unsupervised."

Vicki Spencer of Lorindol Standard Smooths: "I retired as an elementary teacher and for years my Dachshunds would come to my class and interact with my students. They helped me teach science and math and listened as students read to them. I have adults who tell me they still remember the lessons the Dachshunds taught them. I couldn't have asked for more patient, sweet helpers than my standard smooths."

Male or Female?

The only time gender is important is if you are intending to breed the dog. Otherwise, focus on the individual Dachshund's personality. In too many instances, people want female puppies because they assume they will be sweeter and gentler.

No valid basis exists for this assumption. Don't use such a **misconception** to reject a male dog. The real determining factor in any dog's long-term behavior is the quality of its training in relation to its place in the family. Consistency in addressing bad behaviors before they start is crucial.

Female dogs coddled as puppies display more negative behavior and greater territoriality than males. Consider this factor with a grown Dachshund, especially in a rescue situation.

The greatest negative behaviors cited for male dogs are spraying and territorial urine marking.

In the case of purebred purchase, having the animal spayed or neutered is a condition of the purchase agreement. Breeders make pet quality animals available because they do not conform to the accepted breed standard. Such dogs are not suitable for exhibition or for use in a breeding program. Spaying and neutering under these circumstances protects the integrity of the breeder's bloodlines.

The common "wisdom" holds that female Dachshunds are more loyal and affectionate, but males are less problematic to keep. There **seems to be no basis** however to "prove" these assertions. Both genders can be excellent companions and both can be stubborn and difficult. This would seem to indicate the Dachshund personality is a matter of equal opportunity.

Maggie Peat of Pramada Kennels says that new owners should not be focused on male vs. female: "I believe the most important aspect besides general health of a puppy is their temperament. It needs to match the household. So many owners want female puppies, but in many situations a neutered male is a much better fit."

Do You Buy a Puppy or Rescue an Adult Dachshund?

People love puppies for all the obvious reasons. They are adorable, and the younger the dog when you buy him, the longer your time with your pet. At an average lifespan prediction of 15 years, Dachshunds are long lived in relation to their size.

If you do find an adult dog in need of a home, longevity shouldn't be a "deal breaker" in welcoming the animal into your home. As you will learn, Dachshunds have a long adolescence that extends **as much as 18 months**. For this reason, many people prefer to purchase an adult dog. Sadly, many young Dachshunds are surrendered to rescue groups.

I am a huge advocate of all animal rescue organizations. The numbers of homeless companion animals in need of a home stands at shocking levels. To give one of these creatures a "forever" home is an enormous act of kindness. You will be **saving a life**.

Regardless of the dog you choose, please **support** rescue organizations. Such groups are always in need of donations and volunteer hours.

When you do take in a rescue dog, find out as much as possible about the dog's background and the reason for its surrender. Dachshunds are often given up for issues with digging, barking, and aggression toward other dogs.

If these problems are a consequence of environment or treatment, however, it may be possible to correct them. Additionally, pets living with the elderly are frequently surrendered when their owner dies or goes into a care facility. The animals are homeless, but perfectly well-behaved.

Sheila DeLashmutt of ZaDox Dachshunds: "Dogs and especially Dachshunds are loveable additions to families but they are not our children! We disrespect them by not allowing them to fully be the creatures they were intended to be. Dogs need a 'job to do' in order to be fulfilled happy companions. People create 'problem dogs' that fill shelters by asking them to fulfill human emotional needs! Many dogs are asked to be in alpha positions because humans do not understand the nature of the pack. A family is the 'pack' to the dog and the dog needs to understand their JOB in the pack. Truly, the only way dogs achieve the respect they deserve is when we allow them to be the creatures they were created to be.

"Now I don't mean to put you off, but consider some factors please before you make this enormous decision. Just think of how awful it would be for a rescued Dachshund to be abandoned again because his owners could not cope!

"This **isn't a way of getting a cheap Dachshund** and going in with that mentality is so wrong. Even rescue centres may charge an admin fee but on top there are vaccinations, veterinary bills, worming, spaying or neutering to consider. Can you really afford these?

"Many rescued Dachshunds will be suffering the after effects of mistreatment. The poor thing may be unused to much human contact. He might not be housetrained. He may have all sorts of behavioral problems. Can you deal with these? You will need to be an exceptional owner with plenty of time and patience but of course you will truly be rewarded in the long term by saving a Dachshund's life."

Should You Get One or Two?

When you're sitting on the floor surrounded by frolicking Dachshund puppies, your heart may tell you to go ahead and get two. Listen to your head and not your heart! Owning one dog is a serious commitment of time and money, but with two dogs, everything doubles: food, housebreaking, training, vet bills, boarding fees, and time.

Photo Credit: Shirley Ray of Raydachs

I would suggest pacing yourself. Start with one dog and put off buying a second for the future. Multiple Dachshund ownership is quite common, but especially if you are a first-time owner, you need to get accustomed to the Dachshund personality before taking on more than one.

Maggie Peat of Pramada Kennels believes that new owners should get ONE puppy at a time: "My goal is for the puppy to bond with the new owners not each other."

Chapter 2 – Dachshund Dog Breed Standard

The breed standard provides the main blueprint for a number of dog attributes that include a dog breed's physical appearance, his unique moves, and the type of temperament that each breed is expected to have. Created and laid down by the breed societies, dogs that are purebred (pedigree) have their registrations kept by the American Kennel Club and the Kennel Club (in the UK). Registered dogs in a show are usually guided by the rules of the AKC and the Kennel Club and are judged with relation to any ideal

attributes. Breeders approved by the Kennel Clubs have consented to breed puppies based on strict standards of breeding. They simply do not just mate any available male or female (sire or dam).

Photo Credit: Catherine Johnson of Peachtree Kennel

These standards are also aimed at diminishing or even eliminating some genetics that cause illnesses that affect the breed. The Kennel Clubs in your country are the best place to start when you are looking for a puppy. Even if a dog has no registration at the Kennel Club, it doesn't make him a bad dog. Get to know the breed standard before you go out and do some puppy visits so you know what you can expect to see in a well-bred Dachshund.

The breed standard in this chapter has been formulated by the Dachshund Club of America. It is produced verbatim for reference purposes and was established in its current form as of March 1, 2007.

In this book, we have been privileged to have received help and contributions from many members of this club. **Vicki Spencer**, club secretary, tells us more: "The Dachshund Club of America (DCA) is one of the oldest breed clubs in the American Kennel Club dating back to 1895. We currently have over 1,000 members dedicated to promoting and supporting this wonderful breed through sponsoring Dachshund related events which include conformation shows, field trials, earthdog, agility, obedience and rally trials. DCA also financially supports medical research being conducted for the benefit of Dachshunds. Once a year DCA sponsors a national lasting two weeks, offering competitions in all of the above venues plus sponsoring seminars on improving and protecting the breed."

Dachshund Breed Standard USA

General Appearance: Low to ground, long in body and short of leg, with robust muscular development; the skin is elastic and pliable without excessive wrinkling. Appearing neither crippled, awkward, nor cramped in his capacity for movement, the Dachshund is well-balanced with bold and confident head carriage and intelligent, alert facial expression. His hunting spirit, good nose, loud tongue and distinctive build make him well-suited for below-ground work and for beating the bush. His keen nose gives him an advantage over most other breeds for trailing. NOTE: Inasmuch as the Dachshund is a hunting dog, scars from honorable wounds shall not be considered a fault.

Size, Proportion, Substance: Bred and shown in two *sizes*, standard and miniature; miniatures are not a separate classification but compete in a class division for "11 pounds and under at 12 months of age and older." Weight of the standard size is usually between 16 and 32 pounds.

Head: Viewed from above or from the side, the *head* tapers uniformly to the tip of the nose. The *eyes* are of medium size, almond-shaped and dark-rimmed, with an energetic, pleasant expression; not piercing; very dark in color. The bridge bones over the eyes are strongly prominent. Wall eyes, except in the case of dappled dogs, are a serious fault. The *ears* are set near the top of the head, not too far forward, of moderate length, rounded, not narrow, pointed, or folded. Their carriage, when animated, is with the forward edge just touching the cheek so that the ears frame the face. The *skull* is slightly arched, neither too broad nor too narrow, and slopes gradually with little perceptible stop into the finely-formed, slightly arched *muzzle*, giving a Roman appearance. Lips are tightly stretched, well covering the lower jaw. Nostrils well open. Jaws opening wide and hinged well back of the eyes, with strongly developed bones and teeth. Teeth-Powerful canine teeth; teeth fit closely together in a scissors *bite*. An even bite is a minor fault. Any other deviation is a serious fault.

Neck: Long, muscular, clean-cut, without dewlap, slightly arched in the nape, flowing gracefully into the shoulders without creating the impression of a right angle.

Trunk: The trunk is long and fully muscled. When viewed in profile, the back lies in the straightest possible line between the withers and the short, very slightly arched loin. A body that hangs loosely between the shoulders is a serious fault. Abdomen - Slightly drawn up.

Forequarters: For effective underground work, the front must be strong, deep, long and cleanly muscled. Forequarters in detail: Chest - The breast-bone is strongly prominent in front so that on either side a depression or dimple appears. When viewed from the front, the thorax appears oval and extends downward to the mid-point of the forearm. The enclosing structure of the well-sprung ribs appears full and oval to allow, by its ample capacity, complete development of heart and lungs. The keel merges gradually into the line of the abdomen and extends well beyond the front legs. Viewed in profile, the lowest point of the breast line is covered by the front leg. Shoulder blades-long, broad, well-laid back and firmly placed upon the fully developed thorax, closely fitted at the withers, furnished with hard yet pliable muscles. Upper Arm - Ideally the same length as the shoulder blade and at right angles to the latter, strong of bone and hard of muscle, lying close to the ribs, with elbows close to the body, yet capable of free movement. Forearm-Short; supplied with hard yet pliable muscles on the front and outside, with tightly stretched tendons on the inside and at the back, slightly curved inwards. The joints between the forearms and the feet (wrists) are closer together than the shoulder joints, so that the front does not appear absolutely straight. The inclined shoulder blades, upper arms and curved forearms form parentheses that enclose the ribcage, creating the correct "wraparound front." Knuckling over is a disqualifying fault. Feet - Front paws are full, tight, compact, with well-arched toes and tough, thick pads. They may be equally inclined a trifle outward. There are five toes, four in use, close together with a pronounced arch and strong, short nails. Front dewclaws may be removed.

Hindquarters: Strong and cleanly muscled. The pelvis, the thigh, the second thigh, and the rear pastern are ideally the same length and give the appearance of a series of right angles. From the rear, the thighs are strong and powerful. The legs turn neither in nor out. Rear pasterns - Short and strong, perpendicular to the second thigh bone. When viewed from behind, they are upright and parallel. Feet-Hind Paws - Smaller than the front paws with four compactly

closed and arched toes with tough, thick pads. The entire foot points straight ahead and is balanced equally on the ball and not merely on the toes. Rear dewclaws should be removed. Croup- Long, rounded and full, sinking slightly toward the tail. *Tail* - Set in continuation of the spine, extending without kinks, twists, or pronounced curvature, and not carried too gaily.

Gait: Fluid and smooth. Forelegs reach well forward, without much lift, in unison with the driving action of hind legs. The correct shoulder assembly and well-fitted elbows allow the long, free stride in front. Viewed from the front, the legs do not move in exact parallel planes, but incline slightly inward. Hind legs drive on a line with the forelegs, with hock joints and rear pasterns (metatarsus) turning neither in nor out. The propulsion of the hind leg depends on the dog's ability to carry the hind leg to complete extension. Viewed in profile, the forward reach of the hind leg equals the rear extension. The thrust of correct movement is seen when the rear pads are clearly exposed during rear extension.

Rear feet do not reach upward toward the abdomen and there is no appearance of walking on the rear pasterns. Feet must travel parallel to the line of motion with no tendency to swing out, cross over, or interfere with each other. Short, choppy movement, rolling or high-stepping gait, close or overly wide coming or going are incorrect. The Dachshund must have agility, freedom of movement, and endurance to do the work for which he was developed.

Temperament: The Dachshund is clever, lively and courageous to the point of rashness, persevering in above- and below-ground work, with all the senses well-developed. Any display of shyness is a serious fault.

Special Characteristics of the Three Coat Varieties: The Dachshund is bred with three varieties of coat: (1) Smooth; (2) Wirehaired; (3) Longhaired and is shown in two sizes, standard and miniature. All three varieties and both sizes must conform to the characteristics already specified. The following features are applicable for each variety:

Smooth Dachshund: Coat - Short, smooth and shining. Should be neither too long nor too thick. Ears not leathery. Tail - Gradually tapered to a point, well but not too richly haired. Long sleek bristles on the underside are considered a patch of strong-growing hair, not a fault. A brush tail is a fault, as is also a partly or wholly hairless tail. Color of Hair - Although base color is immaterial, certain patterns and basic colors predominate. One-colored Dachshunds include red and cream, with or without a shading of interspersed dark hairs. A small amount of white on the chest is acceptable, but not desirable. Nose and nails-black. Two-colored Dachshunds include black, chocolate, wild boar, gray (blue) and fawn (Isabella), each with deep, rich tan or cream markings over the eyes, on the sides of the jaw and underlip, on the inner edge of the ear, front, breast, sometimes on the throat, inside and behind the front legs, on the paws and around the anus, and from there to about one-third to one-half of the length of the tail on the underside. Undue prominence of tan or cream markings is undesirable. A small amount of white on the chest is acceptable but not desirable. Nose and nails-in the case of black dogs, black; for chocolate and all other colors, dark brown, but self-colored is acceptable.

Dappled Dachshunds - The dapple (merle) pattern is expressed as lighter-colored areas contrasting with the darker base color, which may be any acceptable color. Neither the light nor the dark color should predominate. Nose and nails are the same as for one- and two-colored Dachshunds. Partial or wholly blue (wall) eyes are as acceptable as dark eyes. A large area of white on the chest of a dapple is permissible.

Brindle is a pattern (as opposed to a color) in which black or dark stripes occur over the entire body although in some specimens the pattern may be visible only in the tan points.

Sable - the sable pattern consists of a uniform dark overlay on red dogs. The overlay hairs are double-pigmented, with the tip of each hair much darker than the base color. The pattern usually displays a widow's peak on the head. Nose, nails and eye rims are black. Eyes are dark, the darker the better.

Wirehaired Dachshund: Coat - With the exception of jaw, eyebrows, and ears, the whole body is covered with a uniform tight, short, thick, rough, hard outer coat but with finer, somewhat softer, shorter hairs (undercoat) everywhere distributed between the coarser hairs. The absence of an undercoat is a fault. The distinctive facial furnishings include a beard and eyebrows. On the ears the hair is shorter than on the body, almost smooth. The general arrangement of the hair is such that the wirehaired Dachshund, when viewed from a distance, resembles the smooth. Any sort of soft hair in the outercoat, wherever found on the body, especially on the top of the head, is a fault. The same is true of long, curly, or wavy hair, or hair that sticks out irregularly in all directions. Tail - Robust, thickly haired, gradually tapering to a point. A flag tail is a fault. Color of Hair-While the most common colors are wild boar, black and tan, and various shades of red, all colors and patterns listed above are admissible.

Wild boar (agouti) appears as banding of the individual hairs and imparts an overall grizzled effect, which is most often seen on wirehaired Dachshunds, but may also appear on other coats. Tan points may or may not be evident. Variations include red boar and chocolate-and-tan boar. Nose, nails and eye rims are black on wild-boar and red-boar Dachshunds. On chocolate-and-tan-boar Dachshunds, nose, nails, eye rims and eyes are self-colored, the darker the better.

A small amount of white on the chest, although acceptable, is not desirable. Nose and nails - same as for the smooth variety.

Longhaired Dachshund: Coat - The sleek, glistening, often slightly wavy hair is longer under the neck and on forechest, the underside of the body, the ears and behind the legs. The coat gives the dog an elegant appearance. Short hair on the ear is not desirable. Too profuse a coat which masks type, equally long hair over the whole body, a curly coat, or a pronounced parting on the back are faults. Tail-Carried gracefully in prolongation of the spine; the hair attains its greatest length here and forms a veritable flag. Color of Hair - Same as for the smooth Dachshund. Nose and nails - same as for the smooth.

The foregoing description is that of the ideal Dachshund. Any deviation from the above described dog must be penalized to the extent of the deviation keeping in mind the importance of the contribution of the various features toward the basic original purpose of the breed.

Disqualification: Knuckling over of front legs.

Dachshund Breed Standard UK

The following material is the standard formulated by the UK Kennel Club. It is produced verbatim for reference purposes and was updated August 2014.

General Appearance Moderately long and low with no exaggeration, compact, well muscled body, with enough ground clearance to allow free movement. Heights at the withers should be half the length of the body, measured from breastbone to the rear of thigh. Bold, defiant carriage of head and intelligent expression.

Characteristics Intelligent, lively, courageous to the point of rashness, obedient. Especially suited to going to ground because of low build, very strong forequarters and forelegs. Long, strong jaw, and immense power of bite and hold. Excellent nose, persevering hunter and tracker. Essential that functional build is retained to ensure working ability.

Temperament Faithful, versatile and good tempered.

Head and Skull Long, appearing conical when seen from above; from side tapering uniformly to tip of nose. Skull only slightly arched. Neither too broad nor too narrow, sloping gradually without prominent stop into slightly arched muzzle. Length from tip of nose to eyes equal to length from eyes to occiput. In Wire haired, particularly, ridges over eyes strongly prominent, giving appearance of slightly broader skull. Lips well stretched, neatly covering lower jaw. Strong jaw bones not too square or snipy, but opening wide.

Photo Credit: Tom Sikora of Koradox Kennels

Eyes Medium size, almond-shaped, set obliquely. Dark except in chocolates, where they can be lighter. In dapples one or both 'wall' eyes permissible.

Ears Set high, and not too far forward. Broad, of moderate length, and well rounded (not pointed or folded). Forward edge touching cheek. Mobile, and when at attention back of ear directed forward and outward.

Mouth Teeth strongly developed, powerful canine teeth fitting closely. Jaws strong, with a perfect, regular and complete scissor bite, i.e. upper teeth closely overlapping lower teeth and set square to the jaws. Complete dentition important.

Neck Long, muscular, clean with no dewlap, slightly arched, running in graceful lines into shoulders, carried proudly forward.

Forequarters Shoulder blades long, broad, and placed firmly and obliquely (45 degrees to the horizontal) upon very robust rib cage. Upper arm the same length as shoulder blade, set at 90 degrees to it, very strong, and covered with hard, supple muscles. Upper arm lies close to ribs, but able to move freely. Forearm short and strong in bone, inclining slightly inwards; when seen in profile moderately straight, must not bend forward or knuckle over, which indicates unsoundness. Correctly placed foreleg should cover the lowest point of the keel.

Body Moderately long and full muscled. Sloping shoulders, back reasonably level, blending harmoniously between withers and slightly arched loin. Loin short and strong. Breast bone strong, and so prominent that a depression appears on either side of it in front. When viewed from front, thorax full and oval; when viewed from side or above, full volumed, so allowing by its ample capacity complete development of heart and lungs. Well ribbed up, underline gradually merging into line of abdomen. Body sufficiently clear of ground to allow free movement.

Hindquarters Rump full, broad and strong, pliant muscles. Croup long, full, robustly muscled, only slightly sloping towards tail. Pelvis strong, set obliquely and not too short. Upper thigh set at right angles to pelvis, strong and of good length. Lower thigh short, set at right angles to upper thigh and well muscled. Legs when seen behind set well apart, straight, and parallel.

Feet Front feet full, broad, deep, close knit, straight or very slightly turned out. Hindfeet smaller and narrower. Toes close together, with a decided arch to each toe, strong regularly placed nails, thick and firm pads. Dog must stand true, i.e. equally on all parts of the foot.

Tail Continues line of spine, but slightly curved, without kinks or twists, not carried too high, or touching ground when at rest.

Gait/Movement Should be free and flowing. Stride should be long, with the drive coming from the hindquarters when viewed from the side. Viewed from in front or behind, the legs and feet should move parallel to each other with the distance apart being the width of the shoulder and hip joints respectively.

Coat

Smooth Haired: Dense, short and smooth. Hair on underside of tail coarse in texture. Skin loose and supple, but fitting closely all over without dewlap and little or no wrinkle.

Long Haired: Soft and straight, or only slightly waved; longest under neck, on underparts of body, and behind legs, where it forms abundant feathering, on tail where it forms a flag. Outside of ears well feathered. Coat flat, and not obscuring outline. Too much hair on feet undesirable.

Wire Haired: With exception of jaw, eyebrows, chin and ears, the whole body should be covered with a short, straight, harsh coat with dense undercoat, beard on the chin, eyebrows bushy, but hair on ears almost smooth. Legs and feet well but neatly furnished with harsh coat.

Colour All colours permitted but no white permissible, save for a small patch on chest which is permitted but not desirable. The dapple pattern is expressed as lighter coloured areas contrasting with the darker base. Neither the light nor the dark colour should predominate. Double dapple (where varying amounts of white occurs all over the body in addition to the dapple pattern) is unacceptable. Pied, tricolour and the dilute colours isabella and blue are highly undesirable. Nose and nails black in all colours

except chocolate/tan and chocolate/dapple where they are brown.
Size Ideal weight: 9-12 kgs (20-26 lbs).

Miniature ideal weight; 4.5kgs (10lbs). Desired maximum weight 5kgs (11lbs). Exhibits which appear thin and undernourished should be severely penalised.

Faults Any departure from the foregoing points, including desired body condition, should be considered a fault and the seriousness with which the fault should be regarded should be in exact proportion to its degree and its effect upon the health and welfare of the dog. **Note** Male animals should have two apparently normal testicles fully descended into the scrotum.

Dachshunds in Australia

We are pleased to have **Judy Poulton of Laurieton Dachshunds** involved in this book: "Dachshunds have been in Australia since early in the 20th century with imports predominately from the UK

making the arduous trip by sea then spending time in quarantine on arrival due to the stringent laws requiring disease-free imports. These imported Dachshunds formed a nucleus of outstanding examples of the varieties for many years both in the show ring and as family pets.

"It wasn't until the 80s that the first American Champion Longhair arrived in the country specifically to introduce genetic diversity and renew hybrid vigour into the aging UK/Australian bloodlines of that variety, other varieties followed with great success. The popularity of the miniature varieties has soared in recent years with the standard varieties waning somewhat."

Chapter 3 – Is a Dachshund The Right Dog For You?

When you have moved past the stage of just "window shopping" for a dog and think you're pretty well settled on a Dachshund, there are questions you need to ask, and some basic education you should acquire.

Make no mistake. Dachshunds are not "easy" dogs. They have a complex personality that demands special qualities in their human companions. Dachshund "people" need to be patient, loving, flexible dog owners who are committed to training their pets and creating an environment for them that supports their wellbeing, their best behavior, and gives them emotional security.

You also must understand that you could be signing on for a 15-year (or more) relationship with an intelligent and fairly demanding little dog. Sometimes the only reason Dachshund puppies get away with their non-stop antics is simply that they're so stinking cute!

Dachshund puppies have sharp teeth and they chew on everything, often in excess of other breeds. They like to dig, and they like to bark. They are high-energy little dogs that need a lot of supervision.

These behaviors continue well into adolescence, the same time when the dogs begin to express their natural personality.

Understand from the beginning that your Dachshund will not settle down and become an adult emotionally for 12-18 months.

Many owners give up on their Dachshunds during this crucial period of life, choosing instead to give the dogs away or to abandon them at shelters. If any of this sounds like more than you can handle, then re-evaluate your desire to own a Dachshund!

We asked some of our contributing breeders some questions to help you decide if the Dachshund is the right dog for you.

Is the Dachshund suitable for a person or family that works all day?

Susan Holt of Waldmeister Dachshunds answers: "Dachshunds like company – they are definitely not suitable to be left all day – they are energetic dogs that need their mind (and bodies) exercising – left to their own devices they can be destructive!"

Is the Dachshund breed suitable for a first-time dog owner?

Pat Endersby of Mowbray Dachshunds: "My initial reaction would be no, BUT, so dependent on the new owners. If they take notice of the breeder, and do their research and feel dedicated to the breed it can be very successful, but they would need to learn a lot about the breed first. I have sold to complete newcomers to dog ownership, but they have kept in contact with me through the pup's growth, whilst still with me, discussed many traits and have kept in contact with me through the life of their dog. Obviously very regularly in the early days, which is why it's important to purchase from a knowledgeable breeder."

Some owners seek a breed suitable for barking and offering a guard dog role – how does the Dachshund match up to that role?

Susan Holt of Waldmeister Dachshunds: "Dachshunds have a loud bark that belies their size – they make good dogs for warning when strangers approach and for letting you know someone is at the door although their diminutive size makes them not such a good choice as a deterrent!"

Some breeds can be described as greedy and prone to weight issues, would this apply to the Dachshund?

Pat Endersby of Mowbray Dachshunds: "Yes indeed it does. Most Dachshunds are very greedy and food orientated, which can be helpful during training, always have a tasty reward when a new lesson has been learned, also food reward on recall, but this does all put a big responsibility on the owner. A fat Dachshund is an unhealthy one, and prone to back problems because of excess weight. Owners have to be very strict."

What are the key differences when compared to other breeds?

Pat Endersby of Mowbray Dachshunds: "First and foremost their conformation, they are not long dogs! just a dog with very short legs. The new owner has to realise this from day one. No running up and down stairs, it can put undue strain on the back. They are hounds! Hounds were bred to hunt, and can be selectively deaf when going off on a run. Make sure you have an excellent recall or you may lose your Dachshund. Also I ask new owners, is your garden well fenced? I do not mean a high fence, but secure at ground level, those paws can dig extremely well and the dog will escape. Once grown they can take as much exercise as other breeds but do adore that fireside cuddle."

Do I Need a License?

Before you consider buying your Dachshund, you need to think about whether there are any licensing restrictions in your area. Some countries have strict licensing requirements for the keeping of particular animals.

Even if you are not legally required to have a license for your Dachshund, you might still want to consider getting one. Having a license for your dog means that there is an official record of your ownership so, should someone find your dog when he gets lost, that person will be able to find your contact information and reconnect you with him.

Although there are no federal regulations in the United States regarding the licensing of dogs, most states do require that dogs be licensed by their owners, otherwise you may be subject to a fine.

Fortunately, dog licenses are inexpensive and fairly easy to obtain – you simply file an application with the state and then renew the license each year. In most cases, licensing a dog costs no more than $25.

How to Find and Pick a Puppy

Typically, the first step in finding a specific type of puppy is tracking down a breeder. Thankfully, this is hardly a problem with a breed as popular as the Dachshund. The following tips will help you to make more informed choices during the purchase process.

9 Essential Health Tests You Can Use

Before the "Aw Factor" kicks in and you are completely swept away by the cuteness of a Dachshund puppy, familiarize yourself with some basic quick health checks.

1. Although a puppy may be sleepy at first, the dog should wake up quickly and be both alert and energetic.

2. The little dog should feel well fed in your hands, with some fat over the rib area.

3. The coat should be shiny and healthy with no dandruff, bald patches, or greasiness.

4. The baby should walk and run easily and energetically with no physical difficulty or impairment.

5. The eyes should be bright and clear with no sign of discharge or crustiness.

6. Breathing should be quiet, with no sneezing or coughing and no discharge or crust on the nostrils.

7. Examine the area around the genitals to ensure there is no visible fecal collection or accumulation of pus. If a puppy is dirty from pee or fecal matter then that for me is reason to leave quickly without wasting any more of your time as it indicates poor standards.

8. Test the dog's hearing by clapping your hands when the baby is looking away from you and judge the puppy's reaction.

9. Test the vision by rolling a ball toward the dog, making sure the puppy appropriately notices and interacts with the object.

When you have educated yourself about what to look for in a healthy puppy, move on to visiting breeder websites and speaking over the phone to breeders in whose dogs you are interested. Ask them questions before you schedule a puppy visit. You want to be sure you are going to deal with a reputable breeder.

Photo Credit: Debbie Clarke of Tekalhaus Dachshunds

Some questions you should ask are:

1. Has the puppy been checked by a vet, and do they have a health certificate?
2. Has the puppy had shots and been wormed?
3. What health guarantee do you give with the puppy?

You want to arrive at a short list of potential breeders. Plan on visiting more than one before you make your decision. For now, know that your best option is to obtain a Dachshund from a breeder that is clearly serious about their breeding program and displays this fact with copious information about their dogs, including lots and lots of pictures.

Finding advertisements for Dachshunds in local newspapers or similar publications is **dicey at best**. You may simply be dealing with a "backyard breeder," a well-meaning person who has allowed the mating of two dogs of similar type. There is nothing inherently wrong with this situation, although I do strongly recommend that an independent veterinarian evaluate the puppy before purchase.

All too often, however, if you go through the classified ads you can stumble into a puppy mill where dogs are being raised in deplorable conditions for profit only.

Never buy any dog unless you can meet the parents and siblings and see for yourself the surroundings in which the dog was born and is being raised. If you are faced with having to travel to pick up your dog, it's a huge advantage to see recorded video footage, or to do a live videoconference with the breeder and the puppies.

It is far, far preferable to work with a breeder from whom you can verify the health of the parents and discuss the potential for any congenital illnesses. Responsible breeders are more than willing to give you all this information and more, and are actively interested in making sure their dogs go to good homes. If you don't get this "vibe" from someone seeking to sell you a dog, something is wrong.

This is how **Debbie Clarke of Tekalhaus Dachshunds** prepares her Dachshunds for owners: "I put in an enormous amount of time to ensure all the puppies transition easily into their new home. Our puppies are raised in the home, around all the normal household noises, washing machine, tumble dryer, Hoover, radio — always on. I ensure the puppies get used to all weathers. If it is raining, I will put them out as they need to learn rain is not bad and they can go out to the toilet, play and have fun in it.

"We always put together a folder, a wealth of information of over 20 pages including how to trim feet with photos, all the dos and don'ts, feeding sheet, exercise, toys, a full Kennel Club pedigree and microchip paperwork as they have to be done at 8 weeks before they leave. We prefer to have their first vaccination done too. I also put together a pack, a puppy bed, food bowl, Mason Cash water bowl, blanket, toys, a piece of vet bed that the litter have had during their time with us and a bag of dry complete food and fresh meat (usually chicken) to go home with. We tell all our puppy owners we are here 24/7 365 days a year for them for the life of the puppy."

When to be Cautious

Be **highly suspicious** of any breeder that assures you they have dogs available at all times. It is normal, and a sign that you are working with a reputable breeder, for your name to be placed on a waiting list. You may also be asked to place a small deposit to guarantee that you can buy a puppy from a coming litter. Should you choose not to take one of the dogs, this money is generally refunded, but find out the terms of such a transaction in advance.

Typically females can **only conceive twice a year**, so spring or early summer is the best time to find a puppy. Breeders like to schedule litters for the warm months so they can train their young dogs outside.

Think about what's going on in your own life. Don't purchase a dog at a time when you have a huge commitment at work or there's a lot of disruption around an impending holiday.

Dogs, especially **very smart ones** like Dachshunds, thrive on routine. You want adequate time to bond with your pet, and to help the little dog understand how his new world "runs."

Positives and Negatives of Owning a Dachshund

Talking about pros and cons for any breed always draws me up a little short. It's a very subjective business since what one person may love in a breed another person will not like at all.

I think Jack Russell Terriers are fantastically smart dogs, but they are also the drill sergeants of the canine world. I don't have any desire to give my life over to a dog that will run it at that level. My preference is for more laid back breeds that value a good nap as highly as a rousing game of fetch.

People who love Dachshunds should be ready to talk about their good qualities as well as the challenges they pose for one overriding reason – a desire to see these very special animals go to the best home possible where they will be loved and appreciated. I would rather "put someone off" than see a Dachshund bought and then slowly neglected over time by a less than committed owner.

Pros of Dachshund Ownership

- Courageous and feisty nature
- Expressive personality
- Intelligence
- Manageable compact size
- Physical beauty and variety in coats and sizes
- Lack of a strong odor compared to other breeds
- Good companions
- Have moderate exercise needs
- Good with children if they are raised with them
- Long lifespan

"Possible Negatives" of Dachshund Ownership

- Can be difficult to housetrain
- Some minis can be barkers, standards not at all
- Love to dig and chew
- Seasonal shedding, some hair trimming required with the longhair and wirehair varieties.
- Strong hunting instinct
- Can be protective and territorial
- May be aggressive with other dogs if not raised with them
- May be fearful with children if not raised with them

It is also imperative that new owners understand the many medical problems from which Dachshunds may suffer and their often-epic weight problems. The chapter on health includes a full discussion of potential spinal injuries and other conditions and diseases associated with the breed.

Thank you to **Lorraine and Dave Simmons of Stardox Dachshunds** for their help and suggestions on this section.

How Much Do They Cost?

Prices vary widely. Dachshund puppies for sale from reputable breeders can cost between $850-$3000 depending on whether they are pet quality or show quality. Most breeders do not list prices on their homepages so you need to contact them directly. Good Dachshund breeders usually have a waiting list of prospective owners and **do not sell their dogs to anyone**.

Nora and Paul Price of Samlane Dachshunds says: "Prices in the UK vary from £1000-£2000 for Miniature Smooths and from £900-£1500+ for Miniature Wires and Miniature Longs. Standards are usually between £900-£1200."

Of course it may be possible to browse the Internet or the local classified adverts and see lower prices but **quality breeding comes at a cost** and if a Dachshund puppy is being sold for less, question why.

Photo Credit: Helen 'Dee Dee' Clarke of Deedachs Kennel

Sadly, unscrupulous breeders with almost no knowledge of the breed have sprung up, tempted by the prospect of making easy money. A healthy Dachshund will be an irreplaceable part of your family for the next decade or more. You shouldn't buy an unseen or imported puppy, or one from a pet shop or newspaper! You may end up saving a small amount in the short term only to find you have a puppy that has potential health issues which will cost you thousands more in the long run.

The Kennel Club has conducted research with shocking results. Too many people are still going to unscrupulous breeders, with:

• One third of people failing to see the puppy with its mother
• More than half not seeing the breeding environment
• 70% receive no contract of sale
• 82% were not offered post-sales advice
• 69% did not see any relevant health certificates for the puppy's parents, which indicate the likely health of the puppy

Remember that it isn't about trying to get a "cheap" puppy. Breeder **Sheila Paske of Storybook Dachshunds** explains how much goes into raising puppies: "When I sell a puppy, my primary goal is to find good homes for those I do not keep to move forward in my breeding program. Responsible breeders create a litter to better the breed. Much goes into this process, including pedigree research, progesterone testing to determine the optimal time to breed, flying the bitch to the sire's home, often surgical costs to implant the sperm into the bitch's uterus, ultrasounds, X-rays, and possible surgical costs if a caesarean section is needed. And this does not include the cost and effort that goes into actually raising a litter until it is both physically and emotionally sound enough to go to new homes! As such, putting a price on a puppy is a difficult thing to do. I have personally given away puppies to deserving homes if monetary constraints have made the family unable to buy one. And I do not discuss price until I have determined whether or not I feel the prospective home is worthy."

Obviously we have made clear that finding reputable breeders is your best way to find a puppy but these websites may also help:

American Kennel Club marketplace — http://marketplace.akc.org/
Adopt a Pet — http://www.adoptapet.com
Petango — http://www.petango.com
Puppy Find — http://www.puppyfind.com/
Oodle — http://dogs.oodle.com/

Chapter 4 – Buying a Dachshund

For many people who have never purchased a pedigreed dog, the process can seem daunting and confusing. How do you select a breeder? How do you know if you're working with a good breeder? How do you pick a puppy? Are you paying a good price?

Pet Quality or Show Quality?

First, you need to understand the basic terminology you will encounter to rate puppies that are offered for sale by breeders: pet quality and show quality. Understanding the difference in these designations is often as simple as looking at the offered price. Good

breeders do what they do for one reason: a desire to improve the breed.

When a puppy is not considered to be a superior example of the breed, the dog will be termed "pet quality."

For most of the rest of us, even when the supposed "flaws" are pointed out, all we see is a wonderfully cute and exuberant puppy. For example, see the photo above. This would be considered "pet quality" due to the large white spot on its chest.

You will want a breeder to explain to you why the animal is considered pet quality over show quality, but since reputable breeders don't sell unhealthy dogs, this is not a stumbling block, but rather standard procedure. Show quality animals can cost three times as much or more, so most of us can only afford pet quality pedigree dogs.

The most obvious reason for wanting to buy a show quality puppy is a desire to get involved in the dog fancy and to exhibit your animal in organized competitions. This is a topic I will address more fully later in this book.

Knowing the Key Puppy Stages

0-7 Weeks

Lots of sleep (often up to 18 hours a day), warmth, comfort, and mother's milk-only diet for approximately the first 4 weeks. He learns discipline and manners from his mother, and littermates help with socialization and learning the social rules of the pack. Usually by 7 or 8 weeks the puppies are fully weaned from the mother's milk.

8-12 Weeks

At about 8 weeks the puppies will receive their first vaccine.

A puppy should not leave the litter before 8 weeks, as this could result in negative issues such as shyness. A "breeder" doing this may simply want to cash in and turn over lots of puppies too quickly.

Many responsible breeders will insist on keeping the puppies longer (12 to 14 weeks) to allow the puppy's immune system to become stronger and to allow time for the puppy to learn important life lessons from mom and their siblings. Bite inhibition (covered later) is one of these lessons, that if not learned while in their pack, is much more difficult to teach in their new home.

Now that the brain is developed, he needs socializing with the outside world, otherwise he can become fearful.

12 Weeks Onwards

Your puppy's change to adolescence. Continue exposure to as many different sounds, smells, and people as possible. Begin formal training and obedience, and always praise his good behavior without being too strict or too soft with him.

How to Choose a Breeder

I'm not a great fan of shipping live animals. If possible, try finding a local breeder, or one in reasonable traveling distance. Even if you find a Dachshund breeder online, visit the breeder at least once before you buy. Plan on picking your Dachshund up in person from the breeder.

Note that the Animal Care Welfare Act passed in November 2013 gives new laws/guidelines for breeders who ship. They now need to be **federally licensed** by the USDA.

Be suspicious of any breeder unwilling to allow such a visit or one who doesn't want to show you around their operation. You don't want to interact with just one puppy. You **should meet the parent(s)** and the entire litter.

It's important to get a sense of how the dogs live, and their level of care. When you talk to the breeder, information should flow in both directions. The breeder should discuss both the positives and negatives associated with the dogs.

Nowadays many breeders are home based and their dogs live in the house as pets. Puppies are typically raised in the breeder's home as well. It's very common for Dachshund breeders to use **guardian homes** for their breeding dogs. A guardian home is a permanent family for the dog. The breeder retains ownership of the dog during the years the dog is used for breeding, but the dog lives with the guardian family. This arrangement is great for the dog because once retired from breeding he/she is spayed/neutered and returned to its forever family. There is no need to re-home the dog after its breeding career has ended. There are still breeders who use kennels, but the number of home breeders is quite high and growing.

What to Expect From a Good Breeder

Responsible breeders help you select a puppy. They place the long-term welfare of the dog front and center. The owner should show interest in your life and ask questions about your schedule, family, and other pets.

This is not nosiness. It is an excellent sign that you are working with a professional with a genuine interest in placing their dogs appropriately. Owners who aren't interested in what kind of home the Dachshund will have are suspect.

You want the breeder to be a resource for you in the future if you need help or guidance in living with your Dachshund. Be receptive to answering your breeder's queries and open to having an ongoing friendship.

It is quite common for breeders to call and check on how their dogs are doing and to make themselves available to answer questions.

I strongly recommend you to take your newly purchased puppy to a vet to have a **thorough check-up within 48 hours**. If there are any issues with the health of the puppy, it will be difficult emotionally but worth it to return him to save you from a lifetime of pain as well as the financial costs in vet bills. Good breeders will have a guarantee for this eventuality in their contract.

Lorraine and Dave Simmons of Stardox Dachshunds take this very seriously: "When I talk to prospective puppy homes I always ask them questions about their home life. This way I know what puppy will fit best in that home. That makes it a forever home for a dog. If people know how to pick the 'right puppy for them' it will make it easier. When you go to look at puppies take your lifestyle into consideration. Pick the puppy that will fit in your household. For example, if you have a quiet household and want a lap dog, or just want to take walks with the dog, pick the puppy with the laidback personality. They will be content to sit with you more. If you have active children and want a dog to play fetch with them, pick the busy puppy."

Good Breeders Checklist

1.   Check that the area where the puppies are kept is clean and that the puppies themselves look clean.

2. They don't breed multiple breeds: 2/3 maximum. Ideally they only breed and specialize in the Dachshund.

3. Their Dachshunds are alert and appear happy and excited to meet you.

4. Puppies are not always available on tap but instead they have a waiting list of interested purchasers.

5. They don't over-breed, because this can be detrimental to the female's health.

6. They ask you lots of questions about you and your home.

7. They feed their Dachshunds a high quality "premium" dog food or possibly even a raw diet.

8. They freely offer great specific, detailed advice and suggest they are on hand after the sale to help with any questions.

9. You get to meet the mother when you visit.

10. You are not rushed in and out but get to spend time with the dogs and are able to revisit for a second time if necessary.

11. They provide a written contract and health guarantees.

12. They have health records for your puppy showing visits to the vet, vaccinations, worming, etc. and certificated to show he is free from genetic defects.

13. They clearly explain what you need to do once you get your puppy home.

14. They are agreeable to take the puppy back if necessary.

15. They are part of official organizations or have accreditations.

16. They have been breeding Dachshunds for a number of years.

17. They allow you to speak to previous customers.

18. When selling a purebred (pedigree) Dachshund, the breeder is willing to provide original official AKC or Kennel Club papers to prove registration.

Photo Credit: Carol "Jeani" McKenney of Tarabon Dachshunds

The Breeder Should Provide the Following

In the best cases, transactions with good breeders include the following components.

- The *contract of sale* details both parties' responsibilities. It also explains the transfer of paperwork and records.

- The *information packet* offers feeding, training, and exercise advice. It also recommends standard procedures like worming and vaccinations.

- The *description of ancestry* includes the names and types of Dachshund used in breeding.

- *Health records* detail medical procedures, include vaccination records, and disclose potential genetic issues.

- The breeder should *guarantee the puppy's health* at the time of pick up. You will be required to confirm this fact with a vet within a set period of time.

8 Warning Signs of a Potential Bad Breeder

Always be alert to key warning signs like:

1. Breeders who tell you it is not necessary for you to visit their facility in person.

2. Assertions that you can buy a puppy sight unseen with confidence.

3. Breeders who will allow you to come to their home or facility, but who will not show you where the dogs actually live.

4. Dogs kept in dirty overcrowded conditions where the animals seem nervous and apprehensive.

5. Situations in which you are not allowed to meet at least one of the puppies' parents.

6. Sellers who can't produce health information or that say they will provide the records later.

7. No health guarantee and no discussion of what happens if the puppy does fall ill, including a potential refund.

8. Refusal to provide a signed bill of sale or vague promises to forward one later.

Avoiding Scams

No one wants to support a **puppy mill**. Such operations exist for profit only. They crank out the greatest number of litters possible with an eye toward nothing but the bottom line. The care the dogs receive ranges from deplorable to non-existent. Inbreeding is standard, leading to genetic abnormalities, wide-ranging health problems, and short lifespan.

The Internet is, unfortunately, a ripe advertising ground for puppy mills, as are pet shops. If you can't afford to buy from a reputable breeder, consider a shelter or rescue dog. Even if you can't be 100% certain you're getting a purebred, you are saving an animal in need.

Puppy mills see Dachshunds as profit, but give no thought to breeding integrity.

Again, something is wrong if you can't:

- visit the facility where the puppies were born
- meet the parents
- inspect the facilities
- and receive some genetic and health information

Photo Credit: Travis Wright of RoundAbout Dachshunds

Identification Systems for Pedigree Dogs

Pedigreed dogs may or may not have a means of permanent identification on their bodies when they are purchased. Governing organizations use differing systems. The American Kennel Club recommends permanent identification as a "common sense" practice. The preferred options are tattoos or microchips.

Shirley Ray of Raydachs comments: "All my dogs are microchipped at three months at the time they get their rabies vaccine."

In the United Kingdom, the Kennel Club is the only organization accredited by the United Kingdom Accreditation Service to certify dog breeders through the Kennel Club Assured Breeder Scheme. Under this program, breeders must permanently identify their breeding stock by microchip, tattoo, or DNA profile.

Since 2016, microchipping is compulsory in the UK for all dogs. All puppies sold have to be microchipped by 8 weeks of age, i.e., prior to purchase by new owners.

Any dogs traveling to or returning to the UK from another country can do so under the Pet Passport system, for which microchipping is a requirement. For more information, see http://www.gov.uk/take-pet-abroad. All dogs registered with the Canadian Kennel Club must be permanently identified with either a tattoo or a microchip.

What is the Best Age to Purchase a Puppy?

A Dachshund puppy needs time to learn important life skills from the mother dog, including eating solid food and grooming themselves. For the first month of a puppy's life, they will be on a mother's milk-only diet.

Anne Schmidt of Stardust Dachshunds takes up what happens next: "A mother will start to self-wean her pups when they are about four weeks old. You can tell when she is ready because she will not want to spend much time in the box with them. As the puppies teeth emerge, the dam will be more reluctant to nurse. This is normal and helps her milk production start to slow down. To allow the mother to be with her pups and not be aggravated, we put a t-shirt on her and clip it over her mammary glands so she can still have time with her puppies and start to teach them manners. At this point it is important for the breeder to start supplementing the puppies with a good quality puppy food mixture four times per day. Usually by 7 or 8 weeks the puppies are fully weaned, although, they surely are NOT ready for their new homes yet.

"At about 8 weeks the puppies will receive their first vaccine. Because it is not known exactly when the maternal antibodies from the mother's milk will wear off, a series of vaccines is required. Your veterinarian will give you the best recommendations.

"From the time the puppies are weaned at about 8 weeks until they are ready for their new homes between 10-12 weeks their mother and siblings teach them 'dog manners.' It is highly recommended to keep puppies with their siblings to learn bite inhibition and general rules from their mothers.

"A good breeder will also start basic leash and crate training during the 8-12 week ages. This helps the puppy adjust to its new home much easier!"

How to Choose a Puppy?

My best advice is to go with the puppy that is drawn to you. My standard strategy in selecting a pup has always been to sit a little apart from a litter and let one of the dogs come to me. My late father was, in his own way, a "dog whisperer." He taught me this trick for picking puppies, and it's never let me down.

I've had dogs in my life since childhood and enjoyed a special connection with them all. I will say that often the dog that comes to me isn't the one I might have chosen — but I still consistently rely on this method.

You will want to choose a puppy with a friendly, easy-going temperament, and your breeder should be able to help you with your selection. Also ask the breeder about the temperament and personalities of the puppy's parents and if they have socialized the puppies.

Always be certain to ask if a Dachshund puppy you are interested in has displayed any signs of aggression or fear, because if this is happening at such an early age, you may experience behavioral troubles as the puppy becomes older.

Beyond this, I suggest that you interact with your dog with a clear understanding that **each one is an individual** with unique traits. It is not so much a matter of learning about all Dachshunds, but rather of learning about YOUR Dachshund dog.

Photo Credit: Pat Endersby of Mowbray Dachshunds

Amanda Hodges of Teckelwood Dachshunds adds: "I also recommend asking what health screening has been done for the sire and dam of the litter and what health guarantee goes with the puppy."

6 Great Checks for Puppy Social Skills

When choosing a puppy out of a litter, look for one that is friendly and outgoing, rather than one who is overly aggressive or fearful. Puppies who demonstrate good social skills with their litter mates are much more likely to develop into easy-going, happy adult dogs that play well with others.

Observe all the puppies together and take notice:

1. Which puppies are comfortable both on top and on the bottom when play fighting and wrestling with their litter mates, and which puppies seem to only like being on top?

2. Which puppies try to keep the toys away from the other puppies, and which puppies share?

3. Which puppies seem to like the company of their litter mates, and which ones seem to be loners?

4. Puppies that ease up or stop rough play when another puppy yelps or cries are more likely to respond appropriately when they play too roughly as adults.

5. Is the puppy sociable with humans? If they will not come to you, or display fear toward strangers, this could develop into a problem later in their life.

6. Is the puppy relaxed about being handled? If they are not, they may become difficult with adults and children during daily interactions, grooming, or visits to the veterinarian's office.

Lois and Ralph Baker of Louie's Dachshunds add that "Folks should know the breeders they are dealing with. They should research them and be sure they are reputable breeders. If the breeders have bred two Dachshunds with even mild temperaments, chances are the puppies will be the same."

Submissive or Dominant?

It is something of a myth that dogs are either submissive or dominant. In reality, they are likely to be somewhere in between the two, but it is helpful to understand where they fit in so you know how to deal with them. Watching how they act around their littermates can give you clues.

Submissive dogs:

• Turn away when other dogs stare
• Happy to play with their littermates
• Do not try to dominate them
• May show submissive urination when greeting other dogs
• Allow other dogs to win at tug-of-war
• Provide attention and affection to other dogs
• Back off when other dogs want to take food or toys
• Roll on their backs to display their belly

If a Dachshund shows definite submissive or dominant tendencies, which should you pick? There is no one right answer. You need to choose a puppy that best suits your family's lifestyle.

A submissive Dachshund will naturally be more passive, less manic, and possibly easier to train. A dominant Dachshund will usually be more energetic and lively. They could be more stubborn and difficult to train or socialize, but this needn't be a negative and can be overcome with a little persistence.

Dogs are pack animals, and they are happiest when they have structure and they can follow their nature. Followers want to be told what to do and know what the leaders expect of them. Know that you must be the pack leaders to your Dachshund. He should be submissive even to younger children so aggression and other problem behaviors don't arise.

Chapter 5 – Caring for Your New Puppy

All puppies are forces of nature. That's especially true for an exuberant, sweet, curious, happy, hyperactive, chewing, barking Dachshund! They are little dogs that can get in big trouble before you even know what's happened. The first job ahead of you – and I do mean *before* you bring your new pet home – is to puppy proof the house!

Identify the Dangers

Think of a puppy as a bright toddler with four legs. Get yourself in the mindset that you're bringing a baby genius home, and try to think like a puppy. Every nook and cranny invites exploration. A puppy's inquisitive nose goes into every crevice. Every discovery is then chewed, swallowed – or both!

A Dachshund, especially a young one, will eat pretty much anything, often gulping something down with no forethought.

Take a complete inventory of the areas to which the dog will have access. Remove all lurking poisonous dangers from cabinets and shelves. Get everything up and out of the dog's reach.

If you are not sure about any item, it is best to assume it's poisonous and remove it. Pay special attention to:

- cleaning products
- insecticides
- mothballs
- fertilizers
- antifreeze

Get down on the floor and have a look around from puppy level. Your new furry Einstein will spot anything that catches your attention and many things that don't!

Do not leave any dangling electrical cords, drapery pulls, or even loose scraps of wallpaper. Look for forgotten items that have gotten wedged behind cushions or kicked under the furniture. Don't let anything stay out that is a potential choking hazard.

Tie up anything that could be a "topple" danger. A coaxial cable may look boring to you, but in the mouth of a determined little dog, it could bring a heavy television set crashing down. Cord minders and electrical ties are your friends!

Remove stuffed items and pillows, and cover the legs of prized pieces of furniture against chewing. Take anything out of the room that even looks like it *might* be a toy. Think I'm kidding? Go online and do a Google image search for "dog chewed cell phone" and shudder at what you will see.

Lorraine and Dave Simmons of Stardox Dachshunds tell us about bowel blockages: "This can occur from a Dachshund eating foreign objects they cannot pass. Some Dachshunds are chewers. You must be careful about leaving things on the floor or within reach of them. Rope toys, some hard plastic or rubber bones, towels, or any material with string can be deadly to a dog. I stopped using towels as bedding many years ago as one ate part of a towel and could not pass it. The string acts like a saw in the intestines. This can be deadly. If you suspect your pup or dog has eaten something call your vet immediately as this could require surgery. Your vet may instruct you to induce vomiting to get it up first. If you see that your dog has no interest in eating, or eats and vomits it could have a blockage. They may act lethargic. They may also have a tender belly if you rub it. All these are reason for concern. We recommend replacing bedding with fleece blankets. They have no string and if a dog chews it up it will pass the material."

Plants Can Be Lethal

The list of indoor and outdoor plants that are a toxic risk to dogs is long (over 700!) and includes many surprises. You may know that apricot and peach pits are poisonous to canines, but what about spinach and tomato vines?

The American Society for the Prevention of Cruelty to Animals has created a large reference list of plants for dog owners available at: https://www.aspca.org/pet-care/animal-poison-control/toxic-and-non-toxic-plants

Go through the list and remove any plants from your home that might make your puppy sick. Don't think for a minute that your Dachshund will leave such items alone. He won't!

What to Call Your Dachshund?

Have you thought of a name yet? Here are our best breeder tips:

1. Choose something you're not embarrassed to shout out loud in public.
2. The shorter the better, dogs find names with 1 or 2 syllables easiest to recognize, e.g. Lucky.
3. Long names inevitably end up being shortened so think what they could be now — do you like them?
4. Names starting with s, sh, ch, k, etc. are good because dogs hear high frequency sounds best.
5. Ending with a vowel works well, particularly a short 'a' or a long 'e' sound.
6. Avoid popular and cliché names.
7. Don't go for a name that sounds similar to a command.

8. If you take ownership of a Dachshund that already has a name, keep the new one similar sounding for his sakes.

Bringing Your "Baby" Home

Before you bring your new puppy home, buy an appropriate travel crate and a wire crate for home use. Since the home crate will also be an important tool in housebreaking, the size of the unit is important.

Many pet owners want to get a crate large enough for the puppy to "grow into" in the interest of saving money. When you are housebreaking a dog, you are working with the principle that the animal will not soil its own "den." If you buy a huge crate for a small dog, the puppy is likely to pick a corner as the "bathroom," thus setting back his training.

For **miniature Dachshunds**, a good crate size is the 100 series crate, which measures 21" x 15" x 16" in the Vari Kennel brand. Other brands will vary a bit one way or another.

It is rare for a **standard Dachshund** to weigh much over 30 lbs., so a good crate size is the 200 series crate, which measures 28" x 20.5" x 21.5". For standards over 30 lbs., the 300 size is best.

Put one or two puppy-safe chew toys in the crate for the ride home along with a recently worn article of clothing. You want the dog to learn your scent. Be sure to fasten the seat belt over the crate.

Talk to the breeder to ensure your Dachshund doesn't eat too close to the journey so there is less chance of car sickness, and when he arrives at your home he will be hungry — always a good start!

It is also a nice touch to get an **old rag or towel** from your breeder that has been with the dam. Leave this with your puppy for the first few days, as her scent will help him to settle in more easily.

Take your puppy out to do its business before putting it in the crate. Expect whining and crying. **Don't give in!** Leave them in the crate! It's far safer for the puppy to ride there than to be on someone's lap. Try if possible to take someone with you to sit next to the crate and comfort the puppy while you drive.

Don't overload the dog's senses with too many people. No matter how excited the kids may be at the prospect of a new puppy, leave the children back at the house. The trip home needs to be calm and quiet.

You may need to make a stop depending on the length of journey. He will likely be nervous, so cover the bottom of the crate with newspapers or a towel just in case. **Have water** and give him a drink en route.

As soon as you arrive home, take your Dachshund puppy to a patch of grass outside so he can relieve himself. Immediately **begin encouraging** him for doing so. Dogs are pack animals with an innate desire to please their "leader." Positive and consistent praise is an important part of housebreaking.

Although a gregarious breed, Dachshunds can easily be overwhelmed and nervous in new surroundings. This is especially true of a puppy away from its mother and litter mates for the first time. Stick with the usual feeding schedule, and use the same kind of food the dog has been receiving because their digestive systems cannot cope with a sudden change.

Create a designated "puppy safe" area in the house and let the puppy explore on its own. Don't isolate the little dog, but don't overwhelm it either. Resist the urge to pick up the puppy every time it cries.

Give the dog soft pieces of worn clothing to further familiarize him with your scent. Leave a radio playing at a low volume for "company." At night you may opt to give the baby a well-wrapped warm water bottle, but put the dog in its crate and do not bring it to bed with you.

I realize that last bit may sound all but impossible, but if you want a crate-trained dog, you have to **start from day one**. It's much, much harder to get a dog used to sleeping overnight in his crate after any time in the bed with you.

I also suggest you **take some time off work**. For about two weeks this will be your full-time job! Constant supervision is essential to housetrain your puppy quickly and to give him company while he gets accustomed to his new home, which can be overwhelming to begin with.

Cyndy Senff of Dynadaux Miniatures has this advice: "Additionally what I do is send the puppy with a toy that has been in with the litter. So there is a familiar smell with them. They will learn the owner's smell quickly enough.

"Lastly many breeders will have taught the puppy to stay in a crate at night on their own already. Not always but it is not uncommon. That takes some of the stress out of the first night in the new home."

Remember that your new puppy is essentially a newborn baby — they need a lot of sleep! Puppies need their nap time especially after playing. Also, in the evening keep them up with you so when you are ready to go to bed the pup is as well.

It is also likely for them to whine for the first few days as they adapt to their new surroundings, and they may well follow you around the house constantly. Just handle them gently, make them comfortable and give them peace and quiet and allow them to sleep as much as they need.

They may also shiver and not eat. Of course, this is all very stressful for you, but don't panic. Obviously ensure they are not in a cold place, and put warm blankets in their crate or bed. Your Dachshund will eat eventually. Try taking it away if they are not ready to eat, then the next time you put something down for him, he is more likely to be hungry.

We asked **Mandy Dance of Emem Dachshunds** what essential advice she would give to new owners of Dachshund puppies: "Dachshunds are unique in as much as they are stubborn, clever and bred to work on their own initiative. You don't so much own a Dachshund as they own you!

"The coats give nuances of different characteristics but basically they all think in more or less the same way, i.e. 'how can I turn this situation to my best advantage?' Bearing this in mind you need to be the sort of owner who is willing to compromise! Dachshunds do not tolerate harsh handling and will either withdraw into their shell or become aggressive.

Photo Credit: Debby Krieg of Daybreak Wires.

"They need careful, compassionate understanding and training with food to produce the best results! (Tip: use part of their daily allowance as bribes/treats for use during the day, otherwise they will get too fat very quickly!)

"If you want a dog that thinks he's ten feet tall, has the brains of a Mensa member, who will work alongside you as an equal and who is totally loyal to you, then Dachshunds are the breed for you. Meek little lap dogs they are not! Totally obedient subservient dogs, they are not. Brilliant fun characters that will keep you on your toes at all times they certainly are!

"Don't forget this breed can live well into their teens (I've had one at 18.5 and currently have a 17 year old) and so it has to be the right choice for your way of life. Meeting the breeder and their dogs many times before purchasing your puppy is the way to go in order to prevent mistakes."

The Importance of the Crate

The crate plays an important role in your dog's life. Historically crates have been more popular in America than in Europe, however, this attitude is slowly changing. Don't think of its use as "imprisoning" your Dachshund. The dog sees the crate as a den and will retreat to it for safety and security. Dachshunds often go to their crates just to enjoy quiet time like we humans do from time to time!

When you accustom your dog to a crate as a puppy, you **get ahead** of issues of separation anxiety and prepare your pet to do well with travel. The crate also plays an important role in housebreaking, a topic we will discuss shortly.

Never rush crate training. Don't lose your temper or show frustration. The Dachshund must go into the crate on its own. Begin by leaving the door open. Tie it in place so it does not slam shut by accident. Give your puppy a treat each time he goes inside. Reinforce his good behavior with verbal praise.

Never use the crate as punishment. Proper use of the crate gives both you and your Dachshund peace of mind. In time with some patience and training, he will regard the crate **as his special place** in the house.

Here are our top 10 crate training tips:

1. Dachshunds like to be near their family, so initially they will whine and cry simply because he is separated from you and not because he is in "a cage." Remember that any sort of interaction, positive or negative, will be a "reward" to him, so ignore the whining.

2. Give your Dachshund enough room to turn around in. They appreciate space.

3. Always ensure there is access to fresh water inside the crate.

4. Don't keep them locked up in their crate all day just because you have to go to work — this is unfair.

5. Young puppies shouldn't spend more than 2-3 hours in the crate without a toilet break as they cannot last that long without relieving themselves. This means you should take them out for toilet breaks during the night.

6. Don't place the crate in a draughty place or in direct sunlight where he could overheat. A constant temperature is best. A metal wire crate (compared to plastic) is best so air flows through the gaps.

7. Making the crate his bed from day one is best. Put in some bedding so he feels comfortable and warm at night.

8. Initially to crate train him, put some tasty treats in the crate and leave the door open when he dashes in excitedly! Also be sure to feed him his meals in the crate so he associates it with positive emotions. Don't shut the door yet as that will introduce a negative aspect. Let him roam in and out, being rewarded with treats when he goes into the crate.

9. After a few days, you can begin closing the door for short periods while he is eating. Get ready for some possible whining but remember to stay strong! Some treats pushed through the wire as a reward works well.

10. To begin with just close the door for a minute, no more. In a few days increase the time gradually so he slowly gets accustomed to the door being closed.

So what do our breeders think?

Mandy Dance of Emem Dachshunds says, "I think crate training is good but it should be emphasised that crates are for overnight accommodation and travelling and not for leaving them in during the day while the owner is out. Personally I don't think any dog should be left for more than maximum four hours at a stretch."

Sheila DeLashmutt of ZaDox Dachshunds advises: "Especially for puppies who must stay behind at home while their owner is out on errands, the truly only safe place for a young puppy is in their crate. Young puppies should always be supervised when out of the safety of their crate since they're liable to chew phone or electrical cables which could have serious consequences! Their crate should be utilized as a safe refuge for resting, for naptime or anytime their owner must leave the room."

Lorraine and Dave Simmons of Stardox Dachshunds share the opinion: "The crate is a safe place to put the pup with a treat before you leave the house. This way the pup cannot get into dangerous trouble like chewing an electrical cord, wood molding, or any foreign object that could cause a blockage.

"Then there is going to the bathroom in the house. The crate also teaches the pup to hold it until you return to go out. You take the puppy out FIRST thing when you walk in the door. Young puppies have small bladders and it could take up to 4 months old to hold it all night."

Susan Holt of Waldmeister Dachshunds: "If crates are used people (including children) should respect that if the dog / puppy goes into its crate voluntarily, it is asking for quiet time and should be respected."

Anne Schmidt of Stardust Dachshunds: "I have larger pens for when I am at work with a bed area and a potty area — an x-pen (exercise pen) works great."

Dianne Graham of Diagram Dachshunds: "Dogs are den animals and in the wild they will find or dig a den. At home, giving your pup a toy and a treat when they go into the crate will turn this experience into an enjoyable one and give them the security of a den. Also, pups left loose in the house while the owner is away is simply a recipe for disaster. Coming home to a chewed up couch or, even worse, to a dead pup lying beside a chewed electrical cord isn't what any caring owner wants. It may seem 'mean' to put a pup in a crate while you are away, but it is absolutely necessary!"

Where Should They Sleep?

I have established that I am firmly behind the use of a crate, but you can also have a bed if you prefer, but most importantly — where will they sleep?

I know some new Dachshund owners can't resist having them in their beds, but I strongly suggest not giving into this! Yes, they will whine and cry for the first couple of nights but **this will stop!**

Photo Credit: Andra O'Connell of Amtekel Longhair Dachshunds

Sleeping in your bed could be dangerous, they might wet the bed, and with their short legs **it is dangerous** for them to jump off the bed, and you certainly don't want them wandering down any stairs as their backs are fragile.

I don't recommend it but yes, you could have the crate in the bedroom initially, but why not just start as you mean to go on from day one? Place the crate downstairs I say, and your life will be so much easier once they settle in after a few days.

Go Slow With the Children

If you have children, talk to them before the puppy arrives. Explain that the little dog will be nervous and scared being away from its mother and old home. The initial transition is important. Supervise all interactions for everyone's safety and comfort.

Help children understand how to handle the puppy and to carry it safely. **Limit playtime** until everyone gets to know each other. In just a matter of days, your Dachshund puppy will be romping with your kids.

Introductions with Pets

Introductions with other pets, especially with cats, often boil down to matters of territoriality. All dogs, by nature, defend their territory against intruders. This instinct is strong in Dachshunds.

Don't let a Dachshund puppy and a cat meet face-to-face without some preparation. Create a neutral and controlled interaction under a closed bathroom door first. Since cats are "weaponized" with an array of razor sharp claws, Fluffy can quickly put a puppy in his place. Of course, you want to oversee the first "in person" meeting, but don't overreact. Let the animals sort it out.

With other dogs in the house, you may want a more hands-on approach to the first "meet and greet." Always have two people present to control each dog. Make the introduction in a place that the older dog does not regard as "his." Even if the two dogs are going to be living in the same house, let them meet in neutral territory.

Keep your tone and demeanor calm, friendly, and happy. Let the dogs conduct the usual "sniff test," but don't let it go on for too long. Either dog may consider lengthy sniffing to be aggression. Puppies may not yet understand the behavior of an adult dog and can be absolute little pests.

If this is what is going on, do not scold the older dog for issuing a warning snarl or growl. A well-socialized older dog won't be displaying aggression under such circumstances. He's just putting junior in his place and establishing the hierarchy of the pack.

Be careful when you bring a new dog into the house **not to neglect the older dog**. Also be sure to spend time with him away from the puppy to assure your existing pet that your bond with him is strong and intact.

Exercise caution at mealtimes. Feed your pets in separate bowls so there is no perceived competition for food. (This is also a good policy to follow when introducing your puppy to the family cat.)

What Can I Do to Make My Dachshund Love Me?

From the moment you bring your Dachshund dog home, every minute you spend with him is an opportunity to bond.

Have in mind that your Dachshund has left the warmth and security of his mother and littermates, so initially for a few days he will be confused and even sad. It is important to make the transition from the birth home to your home as easy as possible.

The earlier you start working with your dog, the more quickly that bond will grow and the closer you and your Dachshund will become.

While simply spending time with your Dachshund will encourage the growth of that bond, there are a few things you can do to purposefully build your bond with your dog. Some of these things include:

•   Taking your Dachshund for **daily walks**, during which you frequently stop to pet and talk to your dog. Allow your puppy time to sniff and smell on their walks. He is a hound and loves to explore new scents.

•   **Engaging** your Dachshund in games like fetch and hide-and-seek to encourage interaction.

•   Interacting with your dog through **daily training sessions** – teach your dog to pay attention when you say his name.

•   Being calm and consistent when training your dog – always use **positive reinforcement** rather than punishment.

•   Spending **as much time** with your Dachshund as possible, even if it means simply keeping the dog in the room with you while you cook dinner or pay bills.

Common Mistakes to Avoid

Never pick your Dachshund puppy up if they are showing fear or aggression toward an object, another dog, or person, because this will be rewarding them for unbalanced behavior.

If they are doing something you do not want them to continue, your puppy needs to be gently corrected by you with firm and calm energy, so that they learn not to react with fear or aggression. When the mum of the litter tells her puppies off, she will use a deep noise with strong eye contact, until the puppy quickly realizes it's doing something naughty.

Photo Credit: Susan Holt of Waldmeister Dachshunds

Don't play the "hand" game, where you slide the puppy across the floor with your hands, because it's amusing for humans to see a little ball of fur scrambling to collect themselves and run back across the floor for another go.

This sort of "game" will teach your puppy to disrespect you as their leader in two different ways — first, because this "game" teaches them that humans are their play toys, and secondly, this type of "game" teaches them that humans are a source of excitement. A Dachshund is NOT a toy!

When your Dachshund puppy is teething, they will naturally want to chew on everything within reach, and this will include you. As cute as you might think it is when they are young puppies, this is not an acceptable behavior, and you need to gently, but firmly, discourage the habit, just like a mother dog does to her puppies when they need to be weaned.

Always **praise your puppy** when they stop inappropriate behavior, as this is the beginning of teaching them to understand rules and boundaries. Often we humans are quick to discipline a puppy or dog for inappropriate behavior, but we forget to praise them for their good behavior.

Don't treat your Dachshund like a small, furry human. When people **try to turn dogs into people**, this can cause them much stress and confusion that could lead to behavioral problems.

A well-behaved Dachshund **thrives on rules and boundaries**, and when they understand that there is no question you are their leader and they are your follower, they will live a contented, happy and stress-free life.

Dogs are a different species with different rules; for example, they do not naturally cuddle, and they need to learn to be stroked and cuddled by humans. Therefore, be careful when approaching a dog for the first time and being overly expressive with your hands. The safest areas to touch are the back and chest — avoid patting on the head and touching the ears.

Many people will assume that a dog that is yawning is tired — this is often a misinterpretation, and instead it is signaling your dog is uncomfortable and nervous about a situation.

Be careful when **staring at dogs** because this is one of the ways in which they threaten each other. This body language can make them feel distinctly uneasy.

Habituation and Socialization

Habituation is when you continuously provide exposure to the same stimuli over a period of time. This will help your Dachshund to relax in his environment and will teach him how to behave around unfamiliar people, noises, other pets, and different surroundings. Expose your Dachshund puppy continuously to new sounds and new environments.

When you allow for your Dachshund to face life's positive experiences through socialization and habituation, you're helping your Dachshund to build a library of valuable information that he can use when he's faced with a difficult situation. If he's had plenty of wonderful and positive early experiences, the more likely he'll be able to bounce back from any surprising or scary experiences.

When your Dachshund puppy arrives at his new home for the first time, he'll start bonding with his human family immediately. This will be his **primary** bond. His **secondary** bond will be with everyone outside your home. A dog should never be secluded inside his home. Be sure to find the right balance where you're not exposing your Dachshund puppy to too much external stimuli. If he starts becoming fearful, speak to your veterinarian.

The puppyhood journey can be tiresome yet very rewarding. Primary socialization starts between three and five weeks of age, when a pup's experiences take place within his litter. This will have a huge impact on all his future emotional behavior.

Socialization from six to twelve weeks allows for puppies to bond with other species outside of their littermates and parents. It's at this particular stage that most pet parents will bring home a puppy and where he'll soon become comfortable with humans, other pets, and children.

By the time a puppy is around twelve to fourteen weeks, he becomes more difficult to introduce to new environments and new people and starts showing suspicion and distress.

Nonetheless, if you've recently bought a Dachshund puppy or are bringing one home and he's beyond this ideal age, don't neglect to continue the socialization process. Puppies need to be exposed to as many new situations, environments, people, and other animals as possible, and **it is never too late to start**.

During puppyhood, you can easily teach your puppy to politely greet a new person, yet by the time a puppy has reached social maturity, the same puppy, if not properly socialized, may start lunging forward and acting aggressively, with the final outcome of lunging and nipping.

Never accidentally reward your Dachshund puppy for displaying fear or growling at another dog or animal by picking them up. Picking up a Dachshund puppy or dog at this time, when they are displaying unbalanced energy, actually turns out **to be a reward for them**, and you will be teaching them to continue with this type of behavior. As well, picking up a puppy literally places them in a "top dog" position where they are higher and more dominant than the dog or animal they just growled at.

The correct action to take in such a situation is to gently correct your puppy with a firm yet calm energy by distracting them with a "No," so that they learn to let you deal with the situation on their behalf.

If you allow a fearful or nervous puppy to deal with situations that unnerve them all by themselves, they may learn to react with fear or aggression, and you will have created a problem that could escalate into something quite serious as they grow older.

The same is true of situations where a young puppy may feel the need to protect themselves from a bigger or older dog that may come charging in for a sniff. It is the guardian's responsibility to protect the puppy so that they do not think they must react with fear or aggression in order to protect themselves.

Once your Dachshund puppy has received all their vaccinations, you can take them out to public dog parks and various locations where many dogs are found.

Anne Schmidt of Stardust Dachshunds has an alternate suggestion: "With dog parks, there can be too many uncontrolled big dogs that can chase and hurt the small ones. I prefer to recommend puppy play dates in a fenced yard and puppy manners school."

Before allowing them to interact with other dogs or puppies, take them for a disciplined walk on leash so that they will be a little tired and less likely to immediately engage with all other dogs.

Keep your puppy on leash and close beside you, because most puppies are usually a bundle of out-of-control energy, and **you need to protect them** while teaching them how far they can go before getting themselves into trouble with adult dogs who may not appreciate excited puppy playfulness.

If your puppy shows any signs of aggression or domination toward another dog, you must **immediately step in** and calmly discipline them.

Photo Credit: Amanda Hodges of Teckelwood Dachshunds

Take your puppy everywhere with you and introduce them to many different people of all ages, sizes, and ethnicities. Most people will come to you and want to interact with your puppy. If they ask if they can hold your puppy, let them, because so long as they are gentle and don't drop the puppy, this is a good way to socialize your Dachshund and show them that humans are friendly.

As important as socialization is, it is also important that your Dachshund be left alone for short periods when young so that they can cope with some periods of isolation. If an owner goes out and they have never experienced this, they can destroy things or make a mess because of panic. They are thinking they are vulnerable and can be attacked by something or someone coming into the house.

Audrey Paul of Small Wonders Kennel shares her expertise with us: "A lot of a puppy's personality or temperament is genetic. The puppy will inherit the personality of the parents. That is why it is so important to have solid stable adults in a breeding program. You also have to take into account what the AKC standard for your dog breed's temperament is. Dachshunds are not Labs. They don't run up to every stranger on the street and lick their face off. The AKC standard is that Dachshunds are clever, lively and courageous to the point of rashness, persevering in above- and below-ground work, with all the senses well-developed. Any display of shyness is a serious fault.

"Even though genetics play an important role in a Dachshund's temperament there are also things that a breeder can do to help along a less than ideal personality. There is always a shy one in one of my litters so we spend extra attention on that one when we do early stimulation. We play a CD with noises on it as soon as their ears are open. That way they get accustomed to all noises such as fireworks, cars, a baby crying, things they may not hear in their breeder's home but that they could and most likely will come across in their lifetime and you don't want it to frighten them. While they are with their mother it is a great time to do it because she can reassure them and soothe them — essentially showing them that these noises are nothing to be feared.

"The same goes for everything else we use. We have a crinkle tunnel so they can get used to enclosed spaces and noisy fabric under their feet. We use a slide so they aren't afraid to climb or adventure out from the pack. We use a wobble board when they are steadier on their feet so that any unsteady footing they may encounter during a walk does not make them nervous. We also try to put the puppies on a variety of fabrics to walk on such as hardwoods, linoleum, carpet, grass, and dirt because you don't know what their new owners will have in their home so they need to be accustomed to all of it. They overcome all of these fears when their brain is developing and setting these permanent pathways on what is scary and what isn't.

"So even though temperament is genetic there is a lot that your breeder can and should do to help along a pup that is shyer then the others. And help them become accustomed to things that they may someday run into therefore creating a sound stable Dachshund."

Safety First

Never think for a minute that your Dachshund would not bolt and run away. Even well-adjusted, happy puppies and adult dogs can run away, usually in extreme conditions such as with fireworks, thunder, or when scared.

If he gets lost, it is important he can be identified:

1. Get him a collar with an ID tag because some people may presume that dogs without collars have been abandoned. Note that hanging tags can get caught on things.

2. Put your phone number but not his name on the tag in case he is stolen. A thief will then not be able to use his name. Consider saying, "for reward call."

3. Inserting a microchip below the skin via injection is recommended as this cannot be removed easily by a thief.

4. Recent photos of your Dachshund with the latest clip need to be placed in your wallet or purse.

Train your Dachshund – foster and work with a professional, positive trainer to ensure that your dog does not run out the front door or out the backyard gate. Teach your Dachshund basic, simple commands such as "come" and "stay."

Create a special, fun digging area just for him, hide his bones and toys, and let your Dachshund know that it's okay to dig in that area. After all, dogs need to play!

Introduce your new, furry companion to all your neighbors so everyone will know that he belongs to you.

Know that your Dachshund will not instinctively be fearful of cars so be very careful around roads.

Carol "Jeani" McKenney of Tarabon Dachshunds also says that "A

Dachshund not only may bolt because of loud noises, but that if he sees a rabbit or squirrel or some other sort of prey, sometimes that prey drive is even more compelling than a loud noise. Once they have seen a rabbit or squirrel there is no stopping them especially if they have done some den, field or tracking work.

"Another thing is that Dachshunds can be quite stoic. Lots of times, even when they are ill, they don't show pain. People who use invisible fencing on their dogs forget, or don't realize, that a Dachshund, and I'm sure other breeds, would go right through that fencing if they saw something — rabbit or squirrel — never giving the pain a second thought. Also, if your dog won't go through the fencing, it isn't stopping other animals (fox, fisher cats, etc.) to come into your yard. Once he's out and returned home, now he may not want to come back into the yard, realizing that he will be zapped.

"One last thing, and more 'show' people may do this, is to have their dog DNA tested. It's just another way to secure your dog from someone picking him up (stealing him), for you to prove that he is definitely your dog — especially if he has not been microchipped."

Your Puppy's First Lessons

Don't give a young Dachshund full run of the house before it is housetrained. Keep your new pet confined to a designated area behind a baby gate. This protects your home and possessions and keeps the dog safe from hazards like staircases. Depending on the size and configuration, baby gates retail from $25-$100 / £15-£60.

Housetraining

This section covers the all-important training of your Dachshund to go relieve themselves outside. This is referred to as housebreaking or housetraining and in America it is often termed to as **potty training**.

When the Dachshund is born, they relieve themselves inside their den, with the mother cleaning them up so there is never a scent of urine or feces where the puppies eat, sleep, and live. As they get older, they follow their mother's lead in learning to go outside, so housetraining may already be established when you take your puppy home. If not, they are probably well on the way already. They just need some extra guidance from you.

 We have already stressed the importance of being at home for the first two weeks at least when you bring your pup back from the breeder. If he is left on his own, expect him to eliminate inside the house because at this stage he doesn't realize that the whole house is in effect his den and not the place to eliminate.

Crate training and housebreaking go hand in hand. Dachshunds, like all dogs, come to **see their crate as their den**. They will hold their need to urinate or defecate while they are inside.

Establishing and maintaining a daily routine also helps your dog in this respect. Feed your Dachshund at the same time each day, taking him out afterwards. The feeding schedule dictates the frequency of "relief" breaks. Trips "out" will also decrease as the dog ages.

Don't be rigid in holding your puppy to this standard. Puppies have less control over their bladder and bowel movements than adult Dachshunds. They need to go out more often, especially after they've been active or gotten excited.

On average, adult dogs go **out 3-4 times a day**: when they wake up, within an hour of eating, and right before bedtime. With puppies, don't wait more than 15 minutes after a meal.

If you are keeping your Dachshund puppy in a crate overnight, he will need to be let out once or twice a night as he will not be able to hold it in the whole night until he is aged about four or five months old.

Getting your Dachshund puppy to go outside from day one is best. Your Dachshund will want to keep eliminating in the same spot because the scent acts as **a signal "to go"** in their mind. In time this spot becomes safe and familiar to them. Don't allow them to go on your lawn; being soft, they like this because it feels good under their paws. A discreet corner furthest away from your back door is best, perhaps an area of gravel or, if you live in an apartment, you can use a dog litter tray.

Praise your Dachshund with the same phrases to encourage and reinforce good elimination habits. NEVER punish him for having an accident. There is no association in his mind with the punishment and the incident. He'll have an uncomfortable awareness that he's done *something* to make you unhappy, but **he won't know what**.

Getting upset or scolding a puppy for having an accident inside the home is the wrong approach, because this will result in teaching your puppy to be afraid of you and to only relieve themselves in secret places or when you're not watching.

If you catch your Dachshund puppy making a mistake, all that is necessary is for you to calmly say "no," and take them outside or to their indoor bathroom area. Resist the temptation to scoop him up because he needs to learn to walk to the door himself when he needs to go outside.

Clean up the accident using an enzymatic cleaner to eradicate the odor and return to the dog's normal routine.

Nature's Miracle Stain and Odor Removal is an excellent product and affordable at $5 / £2.97 per 32 ounce / 0.9 liter bottle.

I'm not a big fan of puppy pads because I find puppies like the softness of the pads, which can encourage them to eliminate on other soft areas — such as your carpets!

The following are methods that you may or may not have considered, all of which have their own merits, including:

• Bell training

• Exercise pen training
• Kennel training

All of these are effective methods, so long as you add in the one critical and often missing "wild card" ingredient, which is "human training."

When you bring home your new Dachshund puppy, they will be relying upon your guidance to teach them what they need to learn, and when it comes to housetraining, the first thing the human guardian needs to learn is that the puppy is not being bad when they pee or poop inside.

Photo Credit: Sheila DeLashmutt of ZaDox Dachshunds

They are just responding to the call of Mother Nature, and you need to pay close attention right from the very beginning. If your puppy is making bathroom "mistakes," blame yourself, not your puppy.

Check in with yourself and make sure your energy remains consistently calm and patient, and that you exercise plenty of compassion and understanding while you help your new puppy learn the bathroom rules. Don't clean up after your puppy with them watching, as this makes the puppy believe you are there to clean up after them, making you lower in the dog pack order.

While your Dachshund is still growing, on average, they can hold it approximately one hour for every month of their age. This means that if your 3-month-old puppy has been happily snoozing for two to three hours, as soon as they wake up, they will need to go outside.

Some of the first indications or signs that your puppy needs to be taken outside to relieve themselves will be when you see them:

• Sniffing around
• Circling
• Looking for the door
• Whining, crying, or barking
• Acting agitated

During the early stages of potty training, adding treats as an extra incentive can be a good way to reinforce how happy you are that your puppy is learning to relieve themselves in the right place. Slowly, treats can be removed and replaced with your happy praise, or you can give your puppy a treat after they are back inside.

Lorraine and Dave Simmons of Stardox Dachshunds tell us how long this process can take: "Having both standards and minis I have found that standards (having a big dog personality) house train faster than most minis. I've trained other large breeds such as Great Danes in two weeks but Dachshunds take longer. This is a very common reason for Dachshunds ending up in rescue or shelters - the owners could not house train them.

"There is no timetable for a dog being totally house trained. Yes it can be as quick as two weeks but each pup is an individual and some pick up faster than others. Patience, being consistent on taking them out, and praise when they go is key to success. Also, take note on the times the pup needs to go out. This is helpful with taking them out on their schedule."

Next, now that you have a new puppy in your life, you will want to be flexible with respect to adapting your schedule to meet their internal clocks to quickly teach your Dachshund puppy their new bathroom routine.

This means not leaving your puppy alone for endless hours at a time, because firstly, they are pack animals that need companionship and your direction at all times, plus long periods alone will result in the disruption of the potty training schedule you have worked hard to establish.

If you have no choice but to leave your puppy alone for many hours, make sure that you place them in a paper-lined room or pen where they can relieve themselves without destroying your newly installed hardwood or favorite carpet. Remember, your Dachshund is a growing puppy with a bladder and bowels that they do not yet have complete control over.

Vicki Spencer of Lorindol Standard Smooths: "If the breeder has done her job, the puppy should have a basic understanding of what is expected with potty training. A puppy that has been allowed to soil his sleeping area or go where ever they are will be far more difficult to house train than one who has been taken out routinely and encouraged to potty outside. This is also another reason why I keep my puppies until they are 12-14 weeks. Their bladders are still not mature enough for them to hold their urine all day, but by 12 weeks they can have a good grasp of the whole house training concept."

Bell Training

A very easy way to introduce your new Dachshund puppy to house training is to begin by teaching them how to ring a bell whenever they need to go outside. A further benefit of training your puppy to ring a bell is that you will not have to listen to your puppy or dog whining, barking, or howling to be let out, and your door will not become scratched up from their nails.

Attach several bells to a piece of ribbon or string and hang it from a door handle, or tape it to a doorsill near the door where you will be taking your puppy out when they need to relieve themselves. The string will need to be long enough so that your puppy can easily reach the bell with their nose or a paw.

Next, each time you take your puppy out to relieve themselves, say the word "out," and use their paw or their nose to ring the bell.

Praise them for this "trick" and immediately take them outside. This type of an alert system is an easy way to eliminate accidents in the home.

Kennel Training

When you train your Dachshund puppy to accept sleeping in their own kennel at nighttime, this will also help to accelerate their potty training. Because no puppy or dog wants to relieve themselves where they sleep, they will hold their bladder and bowels as long as they possibly can.

Presenting them with familiar scents by taking them to the same spot in the yard or the same street corner will help to remind and encourage them that they are outside to relieve themselves.

Use a voice cue to remind your puppy why they are outside, such as "go pee," and always remember to praise them every time they relieve themselves in the right place, so that they quickly understand what you expect of them.

Exercise Pen Training

The exercise pen is a transition from kennel-only training and will be helpful for those times when you may have to leave your Dachshund puppy for more hours than they can reasonably be expected to hold it, although we repeat that many of our breeders don't think any dog should be left for more than four hours at a stretch.

Exercise pens are usually constructed of wire sections that you can put together in whatever shape you desire, and the pen needs to be large enough to hold your puppy's kennel in one half of the pen, while the other half will be lined with newspapers, pee pads, or potty pan with pellets.

Place your Dachshund puppy's food and water dishes next to the kennel and leave the kennel door open (or take it off), so they can wander in and out whenever they wish to eat or drink or go to the papers, pan, or pee pads if they need to relieve themselves.

Because they are already used to sleeping inside their kennel, they will not want to relieve themselves inside the area where they sleep. Therefore, your puppy will naturally go to the other half of the pen to relieve themselves.

Marking Territory

Both male and female dogs with intact reproductive systems mark territory by urinating. This is most often an outdoor behavior, but can happen inside if the dog is upset.

Again, use an enzymatic cleaner to remove the odor and minimize the attractiveness of the location to the dog. Territory marking is especially prevalent in intact males. The obvious long-term solution is to have the dog neutered.

Marking territory is not a consequence of poor house training. The behavior can be seen in dogs that would otherwise never "go" in the house. It stems from completely different urges and reactions.

Vicki Spencer of Lorindol Standard Smooths: "I live with 4 intact males who sleep, eat and play together here in the house. I do not have a problem with marking. They know it is totally unacceptable behavior and they don't do it."

Dealing with Separation Anxiety

Separation anxiety manifests in a variety of ways, ranging from vocalizations to nervous chewing. Dogs that are otherwise well trained may urinate or defecate in the house. These behaviors begin when your dog recognizes **signs that you are leaving**. Triggers include picking up a set of car keys or putting on a coat. The dog may start to follow you around the house trying to get your attention, jumping up on you or otherwise trying to touch you.

It is imperative that you understand when you take on a Dachshund that **they are companion dogs.** They must have time to connect and be with their humans. You are the center of your dog's world. The behavior that a dog exhibits when it has separation anxiety is not a case of the animal being "bad." The poor thing experiences real distress and loneliness.

Being with him most of the time can cause him to be over-reliant on you, and then he will get stressed when left alone. As discussed earlier, it is wise to leave him on his own for a few minutes every day so he understands this is normal. You can increase this time gradually.

Remember that to a new puppy, you have now **taken the place of his mother and littermates.** He is completely reliant on you, so it is natural for him to follow you everywhere initially.

As well as puppies, you may also see separation anxiety in rescued dogs and senior (older) dogs.

Fortunately there are things you can do to help. Here are 8 tips:

1. Make sure other family members do things with your Dachshund, e.g. feeding, walking, playing, so he doesn't become over reliant on you.

2. Never punish him. They may do some bad things but this is not their fault and they do not mean to be bad on purpose. You WILL make the situation even worse if you do this.

3. Do your leaving routine such as putting shoes on, getting car keys, etc. and go out and come back almost immediately to build this experience into their brain gradually. Steadily increase the length over time. Do this almost as soon as your puppy comes home, so it won't be such a shock to him when

you really do need to leave him alone.

4. Before you do leave him for real, give him a good walk so he is tired and hopefully sleepy!

5. Leave some toys and things to do so he can occupy himself. Many toys can be filled with tasty treats that should do the trick!

6. When you get back, don't make a big deal or fuss him overly so.

7. Play some soothing music to relax him. Yes this does work!

8. We have talked about crate training. Perhaps put some treats into his crate and leave the door open so he can go into his area he feels most safe in.

10 Tips For Leaving Your Dachshund During The Daytime

Being realistic, most of us have to go to work. While we recommend you take a couple of weeks off when you get your new puppy, the time will come to go back to work during the day.

1. Get a neighbor or friend to come in around lunchtime to spend some time with your pet.

2. Employ a dog walker or come home yourself during your lunch break and take him for a walk.

3. Is there anyone, family, friends, etc. you could leave him with?

4. Exercise generates serotonin in the brain and has a calming effect. Walk him before your work and he will be less anxious and more ready for a good nap.

5. Leave some toys lying around for playtime to prevent boredom and destructive behaviors such as chewing and barking.

6. Make sure that the temperature is moderate. You don't want your dog getting too cold or too hot in the place where you leave him.

7. Don't leave food down all day — he may become a fussy eater. Set specific meal times and remove it after 15-20 minutes if uneaten. This doesn't apply to water — make sure he has access to water at all times.

8. Leave him where he feels most comfortable. Near his crate with the door open is a good option.

9. Play some soothing music on repeat. There are dog-specific audio tracks that claim to ease separation anxiety.

10. Stick to the same routine each day. Don't overly fuss him before you leave OR when you return. Keep it low key and normal.

Photo Credit: Travis Wright of RoundAbout Dachshunds

Further advice comes from **Connie & Gary Fisher of Beldachs Between the Hills:** "They do in fact want to be with you and are very in tune to recognizing those situations where you are going to leave them. They will go through a myriad of antics to avoid being left alone. If you have introduced their crate as a safe haven and a positive place to be, you can make it a fun exercise by using a single word for it, i.e. 'house,' and when they voluntarily go into the crate, reward them with a treat. Minimize the rushing about prior to your departure, tell them to go into their 'house,' reward them with a treat and put on a radio or TV so there is ambient noise. Often a dog will become concerned in a totally quiet environment and that may amplify their anxiety."

Chapter 6 – Food & Exercise

This is perhaps the most **important chapter** in the book because whatever you feed your Dachshund affects the length and quality of his life. Remember too that they are driven by food so will eat pretty much anything put in front of them, and they will eat as much as they can, so it is down to you as to what type of food they eat and how much.

When it comes to what food to serve to your precious Dachshund, the choices seem endless. There is **no one best food** because some dogs need higher fat and protein than others, while some prefer canned over dry.

Bear in mind that food manufacturers are out to maximize their profits, although as a rule you usually get what you pay for, so a  more expensive food is generally more likely to provide **better nutrition** for your Dachshund in terms of minerals, nutrients, and higher quality meats in comparison to a cheap one, which will most likely **contain a lot of grain**.

Even today, far too many dog food choices continue to have far more to do with being convenient for us humans to serve than they do with being a well-balanced, healthy food choice.

We will help guide you through the maze of the supermarket shelves, but in order to choose the right food for your Dachshund, first it's important to understand a little bit about canine physiology and what Mother Nature intended when she created our furry companions. While humans are omnivores who can derive energy from eating plants, our canine companions are **natural carnivores**, which means they derive their energy and nutrient requirements from eating a diet consisting mainly or exclusively of the flesh of animals, birds, or fish — this provides proteins. Yes, proteins can be obtained from non-meat sources, but these are generally harder for the body to digest and have a higher chance of causing dietary intolerances.

Although dogs **can survive on an omnivorous diet**, this does not mean it is the best diet for them. Unlike humans, who are equipped with wide, flat molars for grinding grains, vegetables, and other plant-based materials, canine teeth are all pointed because they are designed to rip, shred, and tear into meat and bone.

Another obvious consideration when choosing an appropriate food source for our furry friends is the fact that dogs are born equipped with powerful jaws and neck muscles for the specific purpose of being able to pull down and tear apart their hunted prey.

The structure of the jaw of every canine is such that it opens widely to hold large pieces of meat and bone, while the mechanics of a dog's jaw permits only vertical (up and down) movement that is designed for crushing.

The Canine Digestive Tract

A dog's digestive tract is short and simple and designed to move their natural choice of food (hide, meat, and bone) quickly through their systems.

Given the choice, most dogs would never choose to eat plants and grains, or vegetables and fruits over meat, however, we humans continue to feed them a kibble-based diet that contains high amounts of vegetables, fruits, and grains with low amounts of meat. Part of this is because we've been taught that it's a healthy, balanced diet for humans, and therefore, we believe that it must be the same for our dogs, and part of this is because all the fillers that make up our dog's food are less expensive and easier to process than meat. While dogs can eat omnivorous foods, we are simply suggesting the **majority** of their diet should consist of meats.

Whatever you decide to feed your dog, keep in mind that just as too much wheat, other grains, and fillers in our human diet is having a detrimental effect on our health, the same can be very true for our best fur friends.

Our dogs are also suffering from many of the same life-threatening diseases that are rampant in our **human society** as a direct result of consuming a diet high in genetically altered, impure, processed, and packaged foods.

Top Feeding Tips

High-quality dog foods provide all the nutrients, vitamins, minerals, and calories that your dog needs. This makes it a lot easier than our human diet where we have to make sure we eat many varieties of foods, and even then, we may be deficient in an important mineral or vitamin. But a word of warning: just because a food is branded as premium **doesn't mean it is**. Essentially the word is meaningless marketing.

Before buying any dog food, read the label. The first (main ingredient by weight) listed ingredients **should be a meat** such as beef, chicken, lamb, **or fish**.

Foods with large amounts of fillers like cornmeal or meat by-products have a **low nutritional value**. They fill your dog up, but don't give him the necessary range of vitamins and minerals, and they increase daily waste produced.

If grains are used, look for **whole grains** (i.e., whole grain corn, whole grain barley) and not cheaper by-products (corn gluten meal, soybean meal).

High-end premium diets avoid grains altogether in favor of carbohydrates such as white or sweet potato.

Avoid artificial colors like Erythrosine, also known as Red No. 3, preservatives such as BHA, BHT, Ethoxyquin, and sweeteners such as sucrose or high fructose corn syrup. Cut out sugars and salt.

AAFCO stands for the Association of American Feed Control Officials. They develop guidelines for the production, labeling, and sale of animal foods. Choose a diet that complies with AAFCO specifications and conducts feeding trials. The label will say: Animal feeding tests using AAFCO procedures substantiate that (name of product) provides complete and balanced nutrition.

Grain free (or raw) is often recommended for the Dachshund. Many are **allergic** to corn, wheat, and some other grains. In addition, no "soy" should be in the dog food – it irritates them!

Wet foods are not appropriate for most growing dogs. They do not offer a good nutritional balance, and they are often upsetting to the stomach. Additionally, it's much harder to control portions with wet food, leading to young dogs being over or under fed.

Controlling portions is important. Give your dog the amount stipulated on the food packaging for his weight and age, and nothing more. If your Dachshund does not eat all of its meal in one go, you may be offering it too much. Many owners ask how many times a day they should feed and the reality is it doesn't matter — what does is the correct feeding amount. You then divide this up by the number of meals you wish to serve. Most owners opt for twice a day for adult dogs.

Stools should be firm, dark brown, and crinkly if portions are correct — if firm but softer towards the end, this is an indication of overfeeding. Stools are a **great indicator** of digestive upsets, so if you notice they are runny or hard, then there is a problem, as is excessive wind or an abnormal amount of feces. These should also not be brightly colored or smelly. Mucous in the stool is a common symptom of irritable bowel syndrome (IBS).

Invest in weighted food and water bowls made out of **stainless steel**. The weights prevent the mess of "tip overs," and the material is much easier to clean than plastic. It does not hold odors or harbor bacteria.

Bowls in a stand that create an **elevated feeding surface** are also a good idea. Make sure your young dog can reach the food and water. Stainless steel bowl sets retail for less than $25 / £14.87.

Leave your Dachshund **alone** while it is eating from its bowl. Don't take the bowl away while he is eating. This causes anxiety, which can lead to **food aggression**.

Do you have more than one dog? I advise **feeding them separately** to completely avoid potential issues. One might try protecting his own food aggressively or try to eat the food designated for the other dog.

Feeding Your Puppy

As Dachshunds age, they thrive on a graduated program of nutrition. At age four months and less, puppies should get **four small meals** a day. From age 4-8 months, **three meals** per day are appropriate. From 8 months on, feed your Dachshund **twice** a day and consider switching to an adult formula.

Vicki Spencer of Lorindol Standard Smooths: "From the very beginning of weaning I put my hands into the puppies' bowls and feed them from my hands. I will take the food bowl from them and immediately offer them a tasty treat, then return their bowl. All of this teaches the puppy it is okay for hands to be around their food. I feel this is a very important life lesson where children are involved. Also, if a puppy grabs something that is not safe for them, they are much more willing to relinquish it."

Be cautious about "free feeding" (leaving some food out at all times) with Dachshunds since the breed is easily **prone to weight gain**. Scheduled feedings in measured amounts are the preferred option and less likely to lead to a fussy eater.

Dachshunds will eat pretty much anything and everything put in front of them, so it is up to you to control their portions!

Begin feeding your puppy by putting the food down for 10-20 minutes. If the dog doesn't eat, or only eats part of the serving, still **take the bowl up**. Don't give the dog more until the next scheduled feeding.

To give your puppy a good start in life, rely on high-quality, premium dry puppy food. If possible, replicate the puppy's existing diet. A sudden **dietary switch** can cause gastrointestinal upset as puppies have sensitive stomachs. Take your pup to the vet if he has diarrhea or he has been vomiting for 48 hours or more.

Maintain the dog's existing routine if practical. To make an effective food transition, mix the existing diet with the new food, slowly changing the percentage of new to old over a period of 10 days.

Some breeders recommend not feeding puppy food. It can be high in protein and actually can cause the puppy to **grow too fast**, thus possibly creating bone growth issues. You may want to switch to a junior or adult food once he leaves puppyhood. Your vet will help decide when best to switch.

If you are eating your evening meal at the same time as feeding your pup, make sure **you eat first**. This keeps to the pack rules, which dictate that you are higher up in the pecking order.

Maggie Peat of Pramada Kennels: "I highly recommend feeding puppies and dogs in the crate/kennel."

Adult Nutrition

The same basic nutritional guidelines apply to adult Dachshunds. Always start with a high-quality, premium food. If possible, stay in the same product line the puppy received at the breeder. Graduated product lines help owners to create feeding programs that ensure nutritional consistency. This approach allows you to transition your Dachshund away from puppy food to an adult mixture, and in time to a senior formula. This removes the guesswork from nutritional management.

Dachshunds should be fed **at least** twice a day (never feed a doxie only once a day) to avoid bloat, which can be fatal. You should also **avoid exercise** immediately before or after eating.

In general, standards get one cup more or less depending on their size; minis get less obviously! If you see your dog getting thinner, it is easy to heap the measuring cup.

Say No to Table Scraps!

Dogs don't make it easy to say no when they beg at the table. If you let a Dachshund puppy have so much as that first bite, you've created a little monster – and one with an unhealthy habit.

Table scraps contribute to weight problems, and many human foods are toxic to dogs. They may be too rich for your Dachshund and cause him to scratch.

Never Feed These to Your Dachshund

Dangerous (some potentially fatal) items include:

- Chocolate
- Raisins and grapes
- Alcohol
- Human vitamins (especially those with iron)
- Mushrooms
- Onions
- Walnuts
- Macadamia nuts

Avoid sausages, sausage meat, and cooked manufactured meats as they can contain sulphite preservatives that can be harmful.

Pat Endersby of Mowbray Dachshunds: "I've often seen it mentioned that garlic is dangerous but a lot of us give garlic three times a week to our dogs, just one small tablet, to help deter fleas. You would have to feed an enormous amount of garlic to poison the dog."

Never feed your Dachshund **cooked bones** as these can splinter and cause internal damage or become an intestinal obstruction. If you give your puppy a bone, watch him. Use only bones that are too large to choke on and take the item away at the first sign of splintering. Commercial chew toys rated "puppy safe" are a much better option.

Never feed your dog from the table or your plate, as this encourages drooling and negative attention-seeking behaviors such as begging and barking.

The BARF/Raw Diet

Raw feeding advocates believe that the ideal diet for their dog is one that would be very similar to what a dog living in the wild would have access to, and these canine guardians are often opposed to feeding their dog any sort of commercially manufactured pet foods.

On the other hand, those opposed to feeding their dogs a raw or Biologically Appropriate Raw Food (BARF) diet believe that the

risks associated with food-borne illnesses during the handling and feeding of raw meats outweigh the purported benefits.

A typical BARF diet is made up of 60-80% of raw meaty bones (RMB). This is bones with about 50% meat, (e.g. chicken neck, back, and wings) and 20-40% of fruit and vegetables, offal, meat, eggs, or dairy foods.

Many owners oversee directly the raw diets, which usually consist of raw meat and bones, with some vegetables, fruits, supplements, and added grains.

Alternatively, you can buy commercial raw diet meals, which come either fresh or frozen. These supply all of the dog's requirements and are usually in a meat patty form.

Many guardians of high-energy, working breed dogs will agree that their dogs thrive on a raw or BARF diet and strongly believe that the potential benefits of feeding a dog a raw food diet are many, including:

- Healthy, shiny coats
- Decreased shedding
- Fewer allergy problems
- Healthier skin
- Cleaner teeth
- Fresher breath
- Higher energy levels
- Improved digestion
- Smaller stools
- Strengthened immune system
- Increased mobility in arthritic pets
- General increase or improvement in overall health
- You control what is in your Dachshund's food bowl
- Avoid ingredients they are allergic or intolerant to
- No preservatives or additives

All dogs, whether working breed or lap dogs, are amazing athletes in their own right, therefore every dog deserves to be fed the best food available. A raw diet is a direct evolution of what dogs ate before they became our domesticated pets and we turned toward commercially prepared, easy-to-serve dry dog food that required no special storage or preparation.

This all sounds good doesn't it? So what **are the downsides**?

- Can be time consuming — less convenient.
- More expensive than other diets.
- Diet may not be balanced unless you are very careful — your Dachshund may become deficient in minerals and vitamins.
- Raw vegetables are often poorly digested by dogs.
- Safety for the elderly and young children — raw diets have been found to contain Salmonella, Campylobacter, E. coli, Clostridium perfringens, Clostridium botulinium, and Staphylococcus aureus. These are all known human and canine pathogens.
- Safety to your Dachshund — some raw foods contain pathogens which can make your dog very sick (even fatally) such as Neospora caninum, found in raw beef, Nanophyetus

salmincola, found in raw salmon, and Trichinella spiralis, found in raw pork.

The Dehydrated Diet (Freeze-Dried)

Dehydrated dog food comes in both raw and cooked forms, and these foods are usually air-dried to reduce moisture to the level where bacterial growth is inhibited.

The appearance of dehydrated dog food is very similar to dry kibble, and the typical feeding methods include adding warm water before serving, which makes this type of diet both healthy for our dogs and convenient for us to serve.

Dehydrated recipes are made from minimally processed fresh whole foods to create a healthy and nutritionally balanced meal that will meet or exceed the dietary requirements for healthy canines.

Dehydrating removes only the moisture from the fresh ingredients, which usually means that because the food has not already been cooked at a high temperature, more of the overall nutrition is retained.

A dehydrated diet is a convenient way to feed your dog a nutritious diet, because all you have to do is add warm water and wait five minutes while the food re-hydrates so your Dachshund can enjoy a warm meal.

There are however some potential disadvantages. It is **more expensive** than other diets (you are paying for the convenience factor), and because of the processing can also **contain more preservatives** than you might ideally want.

Kibble Diet or Canned Food?

While many canine guardians are starting to take a closer look at the food choices they are making for their furry companions, there is no mistaking that the convenience and relative economy of dry dog food kibble, which had its beginnings in the 1940s, continues to make it the most popular dog food choice for most humans. It is basically one of the least expensive choices and is quick, easy, and convenient to serve.

Dry kibble dog food is less messy than canned, easier to measure, and can sit out all day without going bad. It is more economical per pound and is more energy dense than canned food. This is because  dry food is usually only 10% water compared with about 75% water in cans. It takes a much larger volume of canned food to supply the nutrients your dog needs as a can effectively only has 25% food. You also are likely to have to put half-finished cans in your fridge to keep them from going off, and they cause a strong smell unpleasant to some.

Be wary of cheap kibble, which often has high grain content and **is false economy** as they have to eat a lot to get well-nourished.

Canned-food diets do have some **advantages**. Food manufacturers artificially boost the taste appeal of dry kibble by coating it with tempting fats, gravy, and other flavorings. In comparison, the wet and moist food fresh out of a can is much more edible to your Dachshund and often contains more protein, fat, and less additives and preservatives. The texture and smell also have added appeal to their senses!

Food Allergies

Unfortunately, just like humans, Dachshunds are reacting badly to certain foods. It is important to look out for signs, especially **itchy skin**, but also rubbing his face on the floor or carpet, excessive scratching, ear infections, hot patches and rash on the chin and face.

The **most common allergies** are to beef, dairy products, chicken, wheat, eggs, corn, and soy.

How Much to Feed?

We will give you an accurate guide, but there is no definite answer because it depends on a number of varying factors.

Your Dachshund is unique. Even with two the same age, they can have differing metabolic levels with one being very energetic compared to the other, which might be a slouch!

The amount of daily exercise you are able to give your Dachshund is a critical factor because they will burn off more calories the more they do and thus need to eat more without putting on weight.

As a general rule, smaller Dachshunds have faster metabolisms so require a higher amount of food per pound of body weight. Younger Dachshunds also need more food than seniors who by then have a slower metabolic rate.

The type of food you serve is also a factor. There are definitely some lesser quality (low priced) foods that may have the weight (bulk) but offer less in terms of nutrition and goodness.

Be slightly cynical when reading the recommended daily allowance on the labels because they are usually higher than need be. Remember this is from the manufacturer who profits the more your Dachshund eats!

Obesity is now a real problem for many dogs because their owners are unaware they are overweight. Lethargy, high blood pressure, joint problems, heart problems, and diabetes are all much more common in overweight dogs.

Visually you should see that your Dachshund's abdomen is narrower than the chest and hips. You shouldn't be able to see their ribs, but a touch is all you need to feel them. If not, **they are overweight**; if you can see the ribs, they are **underweight**. Looking down from above, you are looking for an "hourglass figure," whereby there is a distinct tapering in at their waist between the abdomen and their hips.

Treats

Treats are a great way to reward your Dachshund for good behavior and also for training purposes, however, there are some cautions to note. Many treats are high in sugar and can contain artificial additives, milk, and fat.

Good quality treats can have nutritional value, but you really don't want to overuse them; I suggest they make up a maximum of 15% of their total daily calorie intake. Try also to use **praise as a reward** instead so you are not always using treats every time he needs rewarding.

Don't forget that treats don't just come out of a packet or box, they can also include normal items such as steamed vegetables, apple slices, and carrot sticks.

A great way to reward and stimulate your Dachshund is a toy that dispenses the treat (food) when he works a puzzle out. The best-known is perhaps the Kong. This chew toy is made of nearly indestructible rubber. Kong sells specially shaped treats and different things you can squeeze inside, but you can stuff it with whatever he likes best.

Nina Ottosson is a genius Swedish pioneer in the world of interactive dog puzzle toys. Her offerings come in a variety of levels of difficulty and in both plastic and wood.

Dianne Graham of Diagram Dachshunds: "Take a hot dog, cut it into 4ths along its length and then chop the long, skinny lengths into lots of little pieces. Cook in the microwave for at least 2 minutes longer than you would normally cook a hot dog. You will have 50+ pieces to use as rewards!"

Ingredients — Be Careful!

Learning to understand the labels on the back of packaging is really important to understand the quality of food you are giving to your beloved Dachshund.

Some manufacturers can use "cute" tricks to **disguise** the amount of grains in their product. They list them separately (to push them down the list order) but added together they can add up to a sizeable amount. The reverse is true, where they add all the meat ingredients together as one so it appears as the first listed ingredient — but check just what else the food consists of!

Although milk contains several beneficial nutrients, it also contains a high proportion of the sugar lactose. As in humans, many dogs have **real difficulties digesting** lactose and as a result, milk products can bring on stomach pains, flatulence, diarrhea, and even vomiting.

When you see meat listed, this refers to the clean flesh of slaughtered animals (chicken, cattle, lamb, turkey, etc.). The flesh can include striated skeletal muscle, tongue, diaphragm, heart, esophagus, overlying fat and the skin, sinew, nerves, and blood vessels normally found with that flesh.

When you see meat by-products listed, this refers to the clean parts of slaughtered animals, not including meat. These include lungs, spleen, kidneys, brain, liver, blood, bone, some fatty tissue, and stomach and intestines freed of their contents (it doesn't include hair, horns, teeth, or hooves).

Don't mistake dry food as being very low in meat content compared to a wet food that lists fresh meat as an ingredient. Fresh meat consists of two-thirds water, so you need to discount the water when doing your comparisons between the two.

The **Guaranteed Analysis** on the label is very helpful as it contains the exact percentages of crude protein, fat, fiber, and moisture.

Don't be scared off if the main ingredient is chicken meal rather than fresh beef. This is simply chicken that is dehydrated, and it contains more protein than fresh chicken, which is 80 percent water. The same is true for beef, fish, and lamb.

Feeding Older Dachshunds

We have a whole chapter on looking after your aging Dachshund, but while we are here, we will make some observations on feeding.

Once your Dachshund passes the age of 11, he can be considered a "senior," and his body has different requirements to those of a young dog — you may notice signs of your dog slowing down, putting on weight, or having joint issues. This is the time to discuss and involve your vet in considering switching to a senior diet.

Because his body's metabolism is slowing down, the adult diet he is on may have too many calories that **cannot be burned off** with the amount of exercise he is capable of. This isn't your fault, so don't feel guilty.

Don't let the pounds pile on. They are much harder to take off than put on, and his weight **literally affects his longevity** as more strain is being put on his internal organs and joints. A senior diet is specially formulated to have a lower calorie count. They tend to be higher in fiber to prevent constipation, which senior dogs can be prone to.

Some breeders suggest supplements such as glucosamine and chondroitin, which assist joints.

The opposite problem is loss of appetite. It may be as simple as needing a change of food, but it could be issues with his teeth. A more moist food may help, but first get his teeth checked by your vet.

Shirley Ray of Raydachs: "I have had several of my dogs to live to be 16 years old. As they start to age to 14 to 15 years they become not as bright in the mind sometimes barking more and not relating to everyday things. I started feeding them Pro Plan Bright Minds. I highly recommend this to aging dogs. You can see a difference for the better within a few weeks. They are more alert and the barking for no reason stops. This is a wonderful product."

What the Breeders Advise on Feeding and Diet

Sheila DeLashmutt of ZaDox Dachshunds advises: "Miniature Dachshunds like most small dogs do best being fed twice per day. We feed a morning and an evening meal of top quality dog kibble covered with water. Dachshunds can be susceptible to bloat due to their deep chests! Adding water to their kibble ensures they consume it along with their kibble lessening the possibility of bloat. Midday snacks are usually small pieces of carrots or apple slices. All of our dogs love these treats! An occasional dog biscuit is also appreciated as well. Dachshunds in general have a tendency to over eat so we always measure their food and we watch their diet carefully. Extra weight on their long backs may predispose them to serious back problems! We never give our Dachshunds table scraps or cooked bones. Bones that are cooked can splinter and cause major stomach upset."

Vicki Spencer of Lorindol Standard Smooths: "I have fed a raw diet for over 27 years. I am fortunate that my guys live long, healthy lives and I attribute it to good genes and a healthy diet."

Susan Holt of Waldmeister Dachshunds: "We feed a completely raw diet prepared into frozen cubes by Nature's Menu. The chunks contain raw meat, ground bone and vegetables and we simply defrost 8 cubes for each of our miniatures twice a day – it is delivered in bulk, is completely natural and seems to suit them really well. No worries about dehydration or extra strain on kidneys, particularly for the oldies – it is also easy to control weight – simply add or remove a cube."

Anne Schmidt of Stardust Dachshunds: "I feed a high quality (4 star) kibble and also supplement with a dry raw dehydrated food, probiotic and brewer's yeast tablets. Standards usually eat about 1 cup kibble per day divided into 2 meals. I have no problem giving my dogs healthy people food also, but everything in moderation. Chicken breast, apples, carrots, and raw green beans are some of their favorites that are healthy and not high in calories."

Maggie Peat of Pramada Kennels: "I feed a high quality dry kibble mixed with water for older dogs. I prefer to feed the food dry as the 'crunchiness' helps keep teeth in good condition."

Debbie Clarke of Tekalhaus Dachshunds: "I feed Purina ProPlan a quality dry kibble. With this I add either fresh meat or (in the UK) Forthglade or Nature's Diet, both 100% meat dog foods of excellent quality. In using both fresh and packaged meats it gives the new puppy owners a choice on how they feed. I always stipulate that the dog should end up being on two meals a day not just one big meal. Much easier on the digestive system too. I do use additives in the form of garlic pearls, Evening Primrose oil, and for the older dogs Glucosamine too. Cod liver oil twice a week although not in the summer as it heats the blood and warm weather is not recommended."

Managing Your Active Dachshund

Dachshunds are high-energy dogs, and although they certainly have the capacity to become lazy couch potatoes, they can also turn

 hyperactive and destructive if bored. They need regular exercise to stay in good health, physically and emotionally!

Your Dachshund likes routine, so establish one and stick to it as much as possible. Just because you have a garden or yard does not mean that you don't need to walk your dog. He needs mental stimulation as well as physical.

Mandy Dance of Emem Dachshunds gives some important advice on specific exercise routines: "When Dachshunds are young, exercise should be limited in as much as pounding pavements should be avoided. Free running for short bursts of a few minutes at a time is fine, and as the puppy reaches around six months the periods of free running can be increased.

"Once muscles and bones are grown when the dog is around twelve months, really they can take as much exercise as the owner wants to give. This should be on a daily basis and not confined to weekends!

"Dachshunds are bred to hunt and dig and so they will naturally be energetic in bursts. They are intelligent and need mental stimulation in addition to physical draining, and may become fractious if kept in too sedentary lifestyles.

"As a rule of thumb around **half an hour free running daily** will be enough to keep your Dachshund toned, and this coupled with a good-sized garden to patrol will keep him on his toes.

"Do make sure where you exercise is safe as Dachshunds will go to ground or take off after rabbits and the like without a backwards glance."

Sue Ergis of Siouxline Dachshunds has specific advice for very young puppies: "I think it is imperative not to exercise puppies under 6 months. I have seen over-exercised baby puppies end up as adults with very unsound joints, as they have been taken for too many long walks. Young puppies have soft bones/joints like a child, and they don't really firm up until 5-6 months old. Over exercising can upset the growth plates that can cause weakness in the elbows, pasterns and stifles. Its fine for them to run round the garden as when they tire they will take themselves to bed but if they are being dragged out on long walks every day, they have no choice but to go along with their owner, hence the damage! By all means socialise puppies by taking them to the park by car, (it is good for them to get used to the car), then let them have no more than about 10 minutes running with other dogs. Make sure the ground is flat, no humps, bumps and uneven ground! Take to friends' houses for socialisation too! When they reach about 5 months then a walk can start occurring but not more than about 20 minutes a day ... build this up slowly until 6 months when they can start going out for lovely long walks in the countryside."

Collar or Harness?

Regardless of breed, I'm not a big fan of using a traditional collar. I wouldn't enjoy a choking sensation and assume my dog wouldn't either, that said, many breeders prefer collars. My current favorite on-body restraints are the harnesses that look like vests. They offer a point of attachment for the lead on the back between the shoulders.

This arrangement directs pressure away from the neck and allows for easy, free movement. Young dogs are less resistant to this system and don't strain against a harness the way they will with a collar.

It's best to take your Dachshunds with you to the pet store to get a proper fit. Sizing for a dog is much more unpredictable than you might think. I have seen dogs as large as 14 lbs. / 6.35 kg take an "Extra Small" depending on their build. Regardless of size, harnesses retail in a range of $20-$25 / £11.88-£14.85.

Judy Poulton of Laurieton Dachshunds adds: "I am very much in favour of a harness especially with a family dog, the firmer support of the harness allows the dog to move freely without pulling on the neck. The firmer support also allows the handler to more easily evade any confrontation from other dogs on a walk."

Pat Endersby of Mowbray Dachshunds is, however, in favor of a collar: "Teach the dog to walk well on a collar and lead. You have no control at all over your dog when on a harness, all you have is a live animal not escaping. He/she will still pull and build up muscles in the wrong places."

Anne Schmidt of Stardust Dachshunds: "We use Martingale collars as the dog cannot slip it over their head, 4-6 feet leash length is perfect for Doxies and leather is best to hold onto as nylon hurts your hands."

Standard Leash or Retractable?

The decision to buy a standard, fixed-length leash or a retractable lead is, for the most part, a matter of personal preference. Some facilities like groomers, vet clinics, and dog daycares ask that you not use a retractable lead on their premises. The long line represents a trip and fall hazard for other human clients.

Indeed **Dianne Graham of Diagram Dachshunds** is not a big fan: "If a dog gets loose, when wearing a retractable lead, it can hit the dog as it runs, which cause the dog to run faster. These leads can be dangerous."

Fixed-length leashes often sell for as little as $5 / £2.97, while retractable leads are less than $15 / £8.91.

Learning to respond to your control of the leash is an important behavioral lesson for your Dachshund. Do not **drag a dog** on a lead or **jerk him**. If your pet sits down and refuses to budge, pick him up. Don't let the dog be in charge of the walk or you'll have the devil's own time regaining the upper hand.

Dachshunds are smart, active dogs. They'll associate the lead with adventures and time with you. Don't be at all surprised if your dog picks up words associated with excursions like go, out, car, drive, or walk.

Dog Walking Tips

Active dogs like Dachshunds are "into" the whole walking experience. This is an excellent opportunity to use the activity to build and reinforce good behaviors on command.

Teach your dog to "sit" by using the word and making a downward pointing motion with your finger or indicating the desired direction with the palm of your hand. Do not attach the lead until your dog complies, rewarding his patience with the words he most wants to hear, "Okay, let's go!"

If your dog jerks or pulls on the leash, stop, pick up the dog, and start the walk over with the "sit" command. Make it clear that the walk ceases when the dog misbehaves.

Praise your dog for walking well on the end of the lead and for stopping when you stop. Reinforce positive behaviors during walks. Your dog will get the message and show the same traits during other activities.

Dianne Graham of Diagram Dachshunds: "To teach the dog to walk with you without pulling, with your dog on your left, start forward with the reward in your left hand, held out in front of the dog. I am facing forward with my hand also facing forward, but the treat is facing the dog. You will have to bend over in order for the dog to see/smell the treat. Walk forward, luring the dog with your hand. After just a few feet, tell him he's a great dog, or give him one word of praise, such as 'yes', in a happy voice, and give him some of your homemade treats. Do this many, many times before you extend your walking to 10 feet or so. Try not to put any pressure on his lead. If he tries to walk ahead of you, turn and go the opposite way."

The Importance of Basic Commands

It is to your advantage to go through a basic obedience class with your dog. By their nature, canines are eager to please, but they need direction. Much of this lies in a consistent routine and command "language."

Experts agree that most dogs can pick up between 165 and 200 words, but they can't extrapolate more than one meaning. If, for instance, your dog barks, you need to use the same "command" in response, like "quiet." If he picks something up, you might say "drop it."

For problem jumping, most owners go with "off" or "down." The point is to pick a set of words and use them over and over to create a basic vocabulary for your dog. Both the word and your tone of voice should convey your authority and elicit the desired response.

This is not a difficult process with a breed whose native intelligence is as advanced as that of the Dachshund. Investigate enrollment in on obedience class through your local dog club or ask your vet about trainers in your area. Start the lessons early in your dog's life by offering him the stability of consistent reactions.

Training should only be done for a few minutes. Make it positive. Remember, he won't learn if he is afraid, so make training fun and upbeat at all times! If you start being frustrated or upset, it is time to stop for the day. Several short training sessions work better than a long one.

Debby Krieg of Daybreak Wires adds: "In general, we train to positively reinforce any desired behavior using small treats when a behavior is done properly — meaning the dog is rewarded for doing the right thing right. This applies to walking, sitting, standing and staying (more important for conformation dogs than sitting).

"I wholeheartedly agree on attending training classes at a young age (referred to as puppy kindergarten here in the USA) but it's important to find a class and instructor who use positive reinforcement training. Dachshunds are very smart but stubborn by nature, so the key to training of any kind is for the dog to want to do what you ask. Rewarding the right behavior makes the dog want to do the right thing."

Dianne Graham of Diagram Dachshunds: "Teaching an emergency come will help if your dog ever gets loose. To teach this, you need a fabulous treat, perhaps a few licks from a jar of baby food meat. Put your dog on a long lead (50 feet). Have someone hold the lead and engage your dog while you walk to the other end. Then call your dog's name and a one word signal in a very loud, excited voice. This call needs to be different from the one you use when you teach a normal come, such as 'here!' or 'now!' When the dog comes, give him lots of praise and several licks from the jar of baby food. Do this many times and practice it weekly. If the time ever comes that your dog is loose or in danger, this emergency come may save your dog's life!"

Play Time and Tricks

Dachshunds have a reputation for being trainable dogs, especially if you cater to their natural burrowing, digging, chasing, and tracking instincts. They like games of fetch, enjoy unearthing "hidden" objects, and are experts at tunneling games like "hand under covers." For more complex tricks, simply extrapolate from the behaviors in which your dog engages just because he is a Dachshund.

Always offer praise and show pleasure for correct responses. This makes training just another form of play – and **Dachshunds love to play**.

The speed with which your dog will amass and destroy a collection of toys may shock you. Avoid soft rubber toys — they shred into small pieces, which the dog will swallow. Opt for rope toys instead or chew toys that can withstand the abuse. You can buy items made out of this tough material in the $1-$5 / £0.59-£2.97 range. Don't buy anything with a squeaker or any other part that presents a choking hazard.

Photo Credit: Vicki Spencer of Lorindol Standard Smooths.

Vicki Spencer of Lorindol Standard Smooths: "Dachshunds are aggressive chewers and unfortunately, some have lost their lives from chewing (and swallowing) off pieces from plastic toys. The plastic pieces accumulate in their stomach where eventually it becomes a medical emergency."

Never give your dog rawhide or pig's ears, which soften and present a choking hazard. Also avoid cow hooves, which can splinter and puncture the cheek or palate.

Playtime is important, especially for a dog's natural desire to chase. Try channeling this instinct with toys and games. If a dog has no stimulation and has nothing to chase, they can start to chase their own tail, which can lead to problems. Dogs that don't get enough exercise are also more likely to develop problem behaviors like chewing, digging, and barking.

Toys can be used to simulate the dog's natural desire to hunt. For example, when they catch a toy, they will often shake it and bury their teeth into it, simulating the killing of their prey.

Allow your dog to fulfill **a natural desire** to chew. This comes from historically catching their prey and then chewing the carcass. Providing chews or bones can prevent your dog from destroying your home. Deer antlers are wonderful toys for a Dachshund, most love them. They do not smell, are all-natural, and do not stain or splinter. I recommend the antlers that are not split: they last longer.

Playing with your dog is not only a great way of getting them to use up their energy, but it is also a **great way of bonding** with them as they have fun. Dogs love to chase and catch balls, but make sure that the ball is too large to be swallowed.

Debbie Clarke of Tekalhaus Dachshunds gives her experiences: "What we do for puppies ... we have a toy mobile over the pen with various soft and hard toys hanging down, also I have a game that you hide food under and they have to move the pieces to get the food ... great to make them use their senses. I buy a variety of toys that speak or squeak — they engage their curiosity and help stop fears developing. Puppies need to experience a variety of different textures whether rubber or plastic soft fabrics.

"On another point when feeding ... I use different bowls and containers ... so plastic, metal, China as they all prefer different things. I had one puppy who would only eat off the floor!

"We, as breeders, all have different ways of doing things but I spend so much time nurturing my puppies so they are well adjusted when they go to their new homes."

Chapter 7 – Grooming

The Dachshund is **not a high-maintenance dog** in terms of grooming. There is seasonal shedding with some hair trimming required with the long hair and wire hair varieties.

Do not allow yourself to get caught in the "my Dachshund doesn't like it" trap, which is an excuse many owners will use to avoid regular grooming sessions. Yes, the Dachshund can be stubborn, but **do not allow** your dog to dictate whether they will permit a grooming session as you are setting a dangerous precedent. In time your Dachshund **will love** to be tickled, rubbed, and scratched in certain favorite places. This is why grooming is a great source of pleasure and a way to bond together.

As **soon as your Dachshund is home**, work on desensitizing him to your touch. This will help when you come to groom him and also when you have to visit the vets. Start slow to begin with and build up the time as he seems comfortable. Touch areas such as his gums and nails so these areas can be maintained by you.

Regular brushing helps your Dachshund in many ways: aerating the coat ensures healthy growth by promoting good blood circulation. It helps to keep grease levels down which can block pores and cause sebaceous cysts. He will also **shed less hair** around your house.

If you don't brush (groom) them, their loose hairs become matted forming heavy wads, which can cause skin complaints and soreness.

The amount of grooming your Dachshund requires will depend on the type of his coat. Smooth-haired require the least maintenance, the long-haired the most. The wire-haired should need stripping (not to be confused with clipping) twice a year.

When your Dachshund is hand-stripped, the dead hair is pulled out, instead of cutting the hair with clippers, so a new wire coat can grow in. This sounds painful but when done correctly it is fine because the wire hair is not attached like our own hair is, so it is much easier to pull out.

Clipping makes the wire coat soft and ruins the texture, so whether your Dachshund is a pet or a show dog you need to strip, not clip, to maintain the recognized breed look!

In terms of brushes, the standard options include:

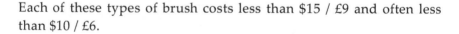

- **Bristle** brushes, which work well with all coats from long to short. They remove dirt and debris and distribute natural oils throughout the coat.

- **Wire-pin** brushes, which are for medium to long coats and look like a series of pins stuck in a raised base.

- **Slicker** brushes are excellent for smoothing and detangling longer hair.

You can often find combination, two-headed brushes. They'll save you a little money and make your grooming sessions easier.

Each of these types of brush costs less than $15 / £9 and often less than $10 / £6.

Anne Schmidt of Stardust Dachshunds: "The Longhair coat should be combed weekly. Spraying the coat with a conditioner before combing will keep it shining and clean. For best results, use a 7.5 inch coarse/fine steel comb. During shedding, the use of a Furminator helps remove the undercoat. In additional to regular nail trims, the feet on a long need the hair trimmed, use a blunt ended safety scissors."

TIP: A friend of mine swears by the **Tangle Teezer** brush. Although it's for women's hair, it apparently works like a charm. She says brushing is now fun and relaxing because her dog believes he is getting a massage.

Brush gently in the direction the coat grows; don't brush "backwards." You will come across matted hair. Apply water or a mat spray and leave it for several minutes. Then use a wide-toothed comb or a mat-splitting tool to get through the tangle. The last resort is cutting this out by scissors.

Grooming/brushing sessions are an excellent opportunity to examine your dog's skin to do a **quick health check**. Look for any growths, lumps, bumps, or wounds. Also have a good look at his ears, eyes, and mouth. Check between paw pads for any balls of matted fur, which can become hard with dirt and grease, causing pain.

Maggie Peat of Pramada Kennels has a handy video on grooming a longhair Dachshund:

https://www.youtube.com/watch?v=Hz-XxgmDTSE

Eyes

Your Dachshund's eyes should be clear and bright, with no excessive discharge apart from that left over from sleeping.

Older dog's eyes may show signs of becoming cloudy; this could be a sign of cataracts, and if you are worried, then it is worth speaking to your vet.

You should wipe their eyes regularly with a warm, damp cloth to remove the buildup of secretions in the corners of the eyes. This can be both unattractive and uncomfortable for the dog as the hair becomes glued together.

If this build up is not removed every day, it can quickly become a cause of **bacterial yeast growth** that can lead to smelly eye infections.

Ears

Your Dachshund's ears should be frequently checked. Look for a dark discharge or regular scratching, as this can be an infection. Affected ears also have a stronger smell than usual.

Dachshunds that have a lot of hair growing inside the ear can struggle with infection, as the hair can prevent normal healthy wax leaving the ear area. The hair inside the ears needs to be cut with safety scissors (blunted end).

Photo Credit: Pat Endersby of Mowbray Dachshunds

Ear mites can become a problem if your dog comes into contact with an infected animal. Too small to be seen by the naked eye, a bad ear mite infestation can cause the dog a lot of unrest and distress. Both infections and ear mites can be diagnosed and treated easily with drops, antibiotics, or both, as prescribed by your vet.

There are many ear cleaning creams, drops, oils, rinses, solutions, and wipes formulated for cleaning your dog's ears that you can purchase from your local pet store or veterinarian's office. You may prefer to use a home remedy that will just as efficiently clean your Dachshund's ears, such as **Witch Hazel** or a 50:50 mixture of hydrogen peroxide and purified water.

Ear powders, which can be purchased at any pet store, are designed to help keep your Dachshund's ears dry while at the same time inhibiting the growth of bacteria that can lead to infections. You may want to apply a little ear powder after washing the inside of your dog's ears to help ensure that they are totally dry.

Bathing

Dachshunds are not known to have a strong "dog" smell, but nevertheless they will need regular bathing, although most are perfectly happy to have baths, and even seem to enjoy the water. If you have a dog with a longer coat, you may choose to hire a professional groomer, but this is certainly not a necessity. Most groomers are quite reasonable, charging in a range of $25-$50 / £15-£30 per session.

For "do it yourself" bathing, just remember **not to get your pet's head and ears wet**. Clean the dog's head and face with a warm, wet washcloth only. Rinse your dog's coat with a mixture of 1tbs shampoo and 2 cups water then pour over dog. Use clean, fresh water to remove all residue. Towel your pet dry and make sure he doesn't get chilled. The rinse is really the most important step of the whole procedure. If any shampoo is left in the coat, it will irritate the skin and lead to "hot spots."

TIP: Try using Chamois cloths to dry your Dachshund. It works great, and they don't have to be laundered as much. They just air dry and can be washed in the washing machine. However, DO NOT put the Chamois in the dryer. I have found that they work much better than towels.

NEVER make the mistake of using human shampoo or conditioner for bathing your Dachshund, because they have a different pH balance than us and it will be too harshly acidic for their coat and skin, which can create skin problems. Always purchase a shampoo for your dog that is **specially formulated** to be gentle and moisturizing on your Dachshund's coat and skin, will not strip the natural oils, and will nourish your dog's coat to give it a healthy shine.

Nail Trimming

Coat maintenance is not the only grooming chore necessary to keep your Dachshund in good shape. Even dogs that walk on asphalt or other rough surfaces often will need to have their nails trimmed from time to time. That said, if you do walk your Dachshund a lot they won't need as much trimming. If nails get too long they can split and get damaged more easily.

If your pet is agreeable, this is a job you can perform at home with a trimmer especially designed for use with dogs. I prefer those with plier grips. They're easier to handle and quite cost effective, selling for under $20 / £11.88.

Never use a regular Dremel™ tool, as it will be too high speed and will burn your dog's toenails. Only use a slow speed Dremel™, such as Model 7300-PT Pet Nail Grooming Tool (approx. $40/£20). You can also purchase the flexible hose attachment for the Dremel which is much easier to handle and can be held like a pencil.

Snip off the nail tips at a 45-degree angle at the point where the nail begins to curve at the tip, before the point where the pink area, referred to as the "quick," is visible. Be careful not to cut too far down, otherwise you will hurt your Dachshund and cause heavy bleeding. If this happens, don't panic. Use a piece of cotton or tissue and hold pressure on it until it stops bleeding. Buy some **styptic powder** just in case. This antiseptic clotting agent causes the vessels to contract, thereby stemming the blood loss. Apply to the nail only, and a warning — initially it will sting your Dachshund.

If you are apprehensive about performing this chore, ask your vet tech or groomer to walk you through it the first time.

Vicki Spencer of Lorindol Standard Smooths: "I have used an  adjustable speed Dremel for years successfully. My guys hop up in a designated chair we call the 'Cookie Chair' (see photo) where they get their nails trimmed using the Dremel. They actually hold their paw out for me to file. After all of their claws are groomed they are rewarded with a cookie."

Cyndy Senff of Dynadaux Miniatures has some thoughts on looking after your Dachshund: "Form follows function. No matter what your Dachshund is going to do in life he needs good structure AND a sound mind. The better the conformation of your pet the better overall health is going to be. That being said, you as the owner have obligations to your pet in keeping him fit and properly maintained. To maximize good health this means not fat and toenails kept trimmed short. Talon toenails have a direct impact on how your dog can walk on his feet. If you do not like doing it, pay a groomer to do it. It is one of the musts for back health. Additionally it is recommended that your Dachshund does not jump off furniture or run down stairs. Both are prime opportunities for mishaps."

Anal Glands

All dogs can suffer from blocked anal glands. The dog may scoot or rub its bottom on the ground or carpet. (You may also notice a foul odor.) If this occurs, the glands will need expressing to prevent an abscess from forming. This is a sensitive task and one that a veterinarian or an experienced groomer should perform.

Helen 'Dee Dee' Clarke of Deedachs Kennel adds: "While I am not a professional groomer, I do make it a regular task to express anal glands. I give a bath to all of my miniature Dachshunds once a month and expressing their glands while in the tub is quick and easy."

Fleas and Ticks

I'm including fleas and ticks under grooming because that's when they're usually found. Don't think that if your Dachshund has "passengers" you're doing something wrong, or that the dog is at fault. This is a part of dog ownership. Sooner or later, it will happen. Address the problem, but don't "freak out."

Do NOT use a commercial flea product on a puppy of less than 12 weeks of age, and be extremely careful with adult dogs. Most of the major products contain pyrethrum. The chemical causes long-term neurological damage and even fatalities in small dogs.

To get rid of fleas, bathe your dog in warm water with a standard canine shampoo. Comb the animal's fur with a fine-toothed flea comb, which will trap the live parasites. Submerge the comb in hot soapy water to kill the fleas.

Wash the dog's bedding and any soft materials with which he has come in contact. Look for any accumulations of "flea dirt," which is blood excreted by adult fleas. Wash the bedding and other surfaces daily for at least a week to kill any remaining eggs before they hatch.

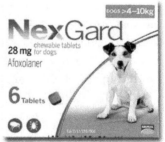

Breeders **Lois and Ralph Baker of Louie's Dachshunds** suggest the following: "We use Nexgard for treatment for fleas and it also treats for heartworms so it is time efficient."

Helen 'Dee Dee' Clarke of Deedachs Kennel adds: "While I do not like to use chemicals regarding my dogs, it seems impossible to use anything else in the battle with fleas, ticks and bugs! For the last decade or so I have used a safe lawn product in my dog yards that kill fleas, ticks, spiders, mosquitoes and more. I go by the directions and don't allow the dogs to go to those yards until after a rain or watering after application, since then I usually do not need to use any other products on the dogs. I do a lawn application the end of March, the end of June and the last one in September."

Photo Credit: Anne Schmidt of Stardust Dachshunds

Anne Schmidt of Stardust Dachshunds: "Dawn dish soap kills fleas and is safe for all ages."

If you find a tick, coat it with a thick layer of petroleum jelly for 5 minutes to suffocate the parasite and cause its jaws to release. Pluck the tick off with a pair of tweezers using a straight motion.

Never just jerk a tick off a dog. The parasite's head stays behind and continues to burrow into the skin making a painful sore.

Chapter 8 – Training and Problem Behaviors

Dachshunds are fun, loving dogs. Because they are food-motivated, they are easy to train. Approach training in a positive way and you should soon have a trained Dachshund.

Introduce him to new sights, sounds, people, and places. Let him interact with other dogs in a controlled environment. There, the dog is safe to deal with fear and timidity without blustering self-defense postures. You'll get a better mannered dog and a greater understanding of how to guide your pet's future interactions.

Previously, I discussed leash training, which is crucial for successful public outings. Rather than avoiding areas with other people and dogs, your goal is to be able to take your dog to such places without incident.

Photo Credit: Connie Fisher of Beldachs Between the Hills

Dachshunds thrive on interaction with their humans and can be happily engaged in interesting public places like parks, walking trails, or beaches that are full of new sights, sounds, and smells. Contrary to what some people think, well-managed outings in varied environments help to create confidence in your dog.

Anne Schmidt of Stardust Dachshunds adds her experience: "Since they are so close to the ground and love to nose surf for food and animal smells, it is very important to start training with attention exercises such as watch me, and in a place with minimal distractions. A Dachshund will 'shut down' with any harsh correction, so having a fun and positive training session is a must - as well as very good treats (mine like liver or chicken)!

"Keep training sessions short and fun and end with a game or a special toy. It is OK to be silly with a Dachshund, they enjoy it!! A high pitch to your voice and lots of love is appreciated. I say 'YES' when they do something right and give an immediate treat.

"Use a separate leash for training and they will learn to tell the difference between this leash and a regular walking leash. Most of all, you will need patience and a sense of humor to train a Dachshund."

Dog Whispering

Many people can be confused when they need professional help with their dog because for many years, if you needed help with your dog, you contacted a "dog trainer" or took your dog to "puppy classes," where your dog would learn how to sit or stay.

The difference between a dog trainer and a dog whisperer would be that a "dog trainer" teaches a dog how to perform certain tasks, and a "dog whisperer" alleviates behavior problems by teaching humans what they need to do to keep their particular dog happy.

Often, depending on how soon the guardian has sought help, this can mean that the dog in question has developed some pretty serious issues, such as aggressive barking, lunging, biting, or attacking other dogs, pets, or people.

Dog whispering is often an emotional roller coaster ride for the humans involved that unveils many truths when they finally realize that it has been their actions (or inactions) that have likely caused the unbalanced behavior that their dog is now displaying.

Once solutions are provided, the relief for both dog and human can be quite cathartic when they realize that with the correct direction, they can indeed live a happy life with their dog.

All specific methods of training, such as "clicker training," fall outside of what every dog needs to be happy, because training your dog to respond to a clicker, which you can easily do on your own, and then letting them sleep in your bed, eat from your plate, and any other multitude of things humans allow, are what makes the dog unbalanced and causes behavior problems.

I always say to people, don't wait until you have a severe problem before getting some dog whispering or professional help of some sort, because "With the proper training, Man can learn to be dog's best friend."

Don't Reward Bad Behavior

It is very important to recognize that any attention paid to an out-of-control, adolescent puppy, even negative attention, is likely to be exciting and rewarding for your Dachshund puppy.

Chasing after a puppy when they have taken something they shouldn't have, picking them up when barking or showing aggression, pushing them off when they jump on other people, or yelling when they refuse to come when called are all forms of attention that can actually be rewarding for most puppies.

It will be your responsibility to provide structure for your puppy, which will include finding acceptable and safe ways to allow your puppy to vent their energy without being destructive or harmful to others.

The worst thing you can do when training your Dachshund is to yell at him or use punishment. Positive reinforcement training methods – that is, rewarding your dog for good behavior – are infinitely more effective than negative reinforcement – training by punishment.

It is important when training your Dachshund that you do not allow yourself to get frustrated. If you feel yourself starting to get angry, take a break and come back to the training session later.

Why is punishment-based training so bad? Think about it this way – your dog should listen to you because he wants to please you, right?

If you train your dog using punishment, he could become fearful of you and that could put a damper on your relationship with him. Do your dog and yourself a favor by using positive reinforcement.

Connie Fisher of Beldachs has the following tips for new owners: "After training several dogs in Agility, Conformation, Earth Dog, Field Trials, Obedience, Rally, and most recently Coursing, I can honestly say, without reservation, that the keys to training a Dachshund can be summed up with the 3P's...Patience (Oh yes!!), Perseverance and of course most importantly, PRAISE. Being hounds, Dachshund do have a mind of their own and one will often find them with their nose on the ground instead of listening to you – particularly those dogs with a great deal of prey drive. But I can guarantee that by taking the time to work with them, Dachshunds will perfect whatever you are trying to teach them fairly quickly. They are very smart and I believe they can get bored easily. So when you are teaching a particular skill, once they have performed it correctly, lavish them with praise (and a special treat will always be well received as well) and come back later or the next day to repeat your training. Make learning fun and be consistent with the commands you use, the tone of your voice, and your body language. Most of all, Dachshunds are a very versatile breed. They can do almost everything and still find their way into your heart as the very best loving companions."

Teaching Basic Commands

When it comes to training your Dachshund, you have to start off slowly with the basic commands. The most popular basic commands for dogs include sit, down, stay, and come.

Sit

This is the most basic and one of the most important commands you can teach your Dachshund.

1.)   Stand in front of your Dachshund with a few small treats in your pocket.

2.)   Hold one treat in your dominant hand and wave it in front of your Dachshund's nose so he gets the scent.

3.)   Give the "Sit" command.

4.)   Move the treat upward and backward over your Dachshund's head so he is forced to raise his head to follow it.

5.)   In the process, his bottom will lower to the ground.

6.)   As soon as your Dachshund's bottom hits the ground, praise him and give him the treat.

7.)   Repeat this process several times until your dog gets the hang of it and responds consistently.

Down

After the "Sit" command, "Down" is the next logical command to teach because it is a progression from "Sit."

1.)   Kneel in front of your Dachshund with a few small treats in your pocket.

2.)   Hold one treat in your dominant hand and give your Dachshund the "Sit" command.

3.)   Reward your Dachshund for sitting, then give him the "Down" command.

4.)   Quickly move the treat down to the floor between your

Dachshund's paws.

5.)   Your dog will follow the treat and should lie down to retrieve it.

6.)   Praise and reward your Dachshund when he lies down.

7.)   Repeat this process several times until your dog gets the hang of it and responds consistently.

Come

It is very important that your Dachshund responds to a "Come" command, because there may come a time when you need to get his attention and call him to your side during a dangerous situation (such as him running around too close to traffic).

1.)   Put your Dachshund on a short leash and stand in front of him.

2.)   Give your Dachshund the "Come" command, then quickly take a few steps backward away from him.

3.)   Clap your hands and act excited, but do not repeat the "Come" command.

4.)   Keep moving backwards in small steps until your Dachshund follows and comes to you.

5.)   Praise and reward your Dachshund and repeat the process.

6.)   Over time, you can use a longer leash or take your Dachshund off the leash entirely.

7.)   You can also start by standing further from your Dachshund when you give the "Come" command.

8.)   If your Dachshund doesn't come to you immediately, you can use the leash to pull him toward you.

Stay

This command is very important because it teaches your Dachshund discipline – not only does it teach your Dachshund to stay, but it also forces him to listen and pay attention to you.

1.)   Find a friend to help you with this training session.

2.)   Have your friend hold your Dachshund on the leash while you stand in front of the dog.

3.)   Give your Dachshund the "Sit" command and reward him for responding correctly.

4.)   Give your dog the "Stay" command while holding your hand out like a "Stop" sign.

5.)   Take a few steps backward away from your dog and pause for 1 to 2 seconds.

6.)   Step back toward your Dachshund, then praise and reward your dog.

7.)   Repeat the process several times, then start moving back a little further before you return to your dog.

Beyond Basic Training

Once your Dachshund has a firm grasp on the basics, you can move on to teaching him additional commands. You can also add distractions to the equation to reinforce your dog's mastery of the commands. The end goal is to ensure that your Dachshund responds to your command each and every time – regardless of distractions and anything else he might rather be doing. This is incredibly important, because there may come a time when your dog is in a dangerous situation and if he doesn't respond to your command, he could get hurt.

After your Dachshund has started to respond correctly to the basic commands on a regular basis, you can start to incorporate distractions.

If you previously conducted your training sessions indoors, you might consider moving them outside where your dog could be distracted by various sights, smells, and sounds.

One thing you might try is to give your dog the Stay command and

then toss a toy nearby that will tempt him to break his Stay. Start by tossing the toy at a good distance from him and wait a few seconds before you release him to play. Eventually you will be able to toss a toy right next to your dog without him breaking his Stay until you give him permission to do so.

Photo Credit: Lucy Granowicz of Von Links Dachshunds

Incorporating Hand Signals

Teaching your Dachshund to respond to hand signals in addition to verbal commands is very useful – you never know when you will be in a situation where your dog might not be able to hear you.

To start out, choose your dominant hand to give the hand signals, and hold a small treat in that hand while you are training your dog – this will encourage your dog to focus on your hand during training, and it will help to cement the connection between the command and the hand signal.

To begin, give your dog the Sit or Down command while holding the treat in your dominant hand and give the appropriate hand signal – for Sit you might try a closed fist and for Down, you might place your hand flat, parallel to the ground.

When your dog responds correctly, give him the treat. You will need to repeat this process many times in order for your dog to form a connection between both the verbal command and the hand signal with the desired behavior.

Eventually, you can start to remove the verbal command from the equation – use the hand gesture every time, but start to use the verbal command only half the time.

Once your dog gets the hang of this, you should start to remove the food reward from the equation. Continue to give your dog the hand signal for each command, and occasionally use the verbal command just to remind him.

You should start to phase out the food rewards, however, by offering them only half the time. Progressively lessen the use of the food reward, but continue to praise your dog for performing the behavior correctly so he learns to repeat it.

Teaching Distance Commands

In addition to getting your dog to respond to hand signals, it is also useful to teach him to respond to your commands even when you are not directly next to him.

This may come in handy if your dog is running around outside and gets too close to the street – you should be able to give him a Sit or Down command so he stops before he gets into a dangerous situation.

Teaching your dog distance commands is not difficult, but it does require some time and patience.

To start, give your Dachshund a brief refresher course of the basic commands while you are standing or kneeling right next to him.

Next, give your dog the Sit and Stay commands, then move a few feet away before you give the Come command.

Repeat this process, increasing the distance between you and your dog before giving him the Come command. Be sure to praise and reward your dog for responding appropriately when he does so.

Once your dog gets the hang of coming on command from a distance, you can start to incorporate other commands.

One method of doing so is to teach your dog to sit when you grab his collar. To do so, let your dog wander freely and every once in a while walk up and grab his collar while giving the Sit command.

After a few repetitions, your dog should begin to respond with a Sit when you grab his collar, even if you do not give the command.

Gradually, you can increase the distance from which you come to grab his collar and give him the command.

After your dog starts to respond consistently when you come from a distance to grab his collar, you can start giving the Sit command without moving toward him.

It may take your dog a few times to get the hang of it, so be patient. If your dog doesn't sit right away, calmly walk up to him and repeat the Sit command, but do not grab his collar this time.

Eventually, your dog will get the hang of it, and you can start to practice using other commands like Down and Stay from a distance.

Clicker Training

When it comes to training your Dachshund, you are going to be most successful if you maintain consistency. Dachshunds have a tendency to be a little stubborn, so unless you are very clear with your dog about what your expectations are, he may simply decide not to follow your commands.

A simple way to achieve consistency in training your Dachshund is to use the principles of clicker training. Clicker training involves using a small handheld device that makes a clicking noise when you press it between your fingers.

Clicker training is based on the theory of operant conditioning, which helps your dog to make the connection between the desired behavior and the offering of a reward.

Dachshunds have a natural desire to please, so if they learn that a certain behavior earns your approval, they will be eager to repeat it – clicker training is a great way to help your dog quickly identify the particular behavior you want him to repeat.

All you have to do is give your Dachshund a command and, as soon as he performs the behavior, you use the clicker. After you use the clicker, give your dog the reward as you would with any form of positive reinforcement training.

Some of the benefits of clicker training include:

• 	Very easy to implement – all you need is the clicker.
• 	Helps your dog form a connection between the command and the desired behavior more quickly.
• 	You only need to use the clicker until your dog makes the connection, then you can stop.
• 	May help to keep your dog's attention more effectively if he hears the noise.

Clicker training is just one method of positive reinforcement training that you can consider for training your Dachshund.

No matter what method you choose, it is important that you maintain consistency and always praise and reward your dog for responding to your commands correctly so he learns to repeat the behavior.

First Tricks

When teaching your Dachshund their first tricks, in order to give them extra incentive, find a small treat that they would do anything to get, and give the treat as a reward to help solidify a good performance.

Most dogs will be extra attentive during training sessions when they know that they will be rewarded with their favorite treats.

If your Dachshund is less than six months old when you begin teaching them tricks, keep your training sessions short (no more than 5 or 10 minutes) and make the sessions lots of fun.

As your Dachshund becomes an adult, you can extend your sessions because they will be able to maintain their focus for longer periods of time.

Playing Dead

Once your Dachshund knows the command to "lie down," which should be one of the basic obedience commands he learns at "school," getting him to "play dead" is simple.

Once the dog is lying down, hold a treat in front of your pet close enough for him to smell it. Move the treat in circles toward the floor giving your Dachshund the command, "Play Dead."

The motion should encourage the dog to roll over on his back. As soon as he achieves the correct position, praise him and give him the treat. Dachshunds love treats so much, it won't take your pet long to put it all together and execute the maneuver on command.

Shake a Paw

Who doesn't love a dog who knows how to shake a paw? This is one of the easiest tricks to teach your Dachshund.

Practice every day until they are 100% reliable with this trick, and then it will be time to add another trick to their repertoire.

Most dogs are naturally either right or left pawed. If you know which paw your dog favors, ask them to shake this paw.

Find a quiet place to practice, without noisy distractions or other pets, and stand or sit in front of your dog. Place them in the sitting position and hold a treat in your left hand.

Say the command "Shake" while putting your right hand behind their left or right paw and pulling the paw gently toward yourself until you are holding their paw in your hand. Immediately praise them and give them the treat.

Most dogs will learn the "Shake" trick very quickly, and in no time at all, once you put out your hand, your Dachshund will immediately lift their paw and put it into your hand without your assistance or any verbal cue.

Give Me Five

The next trick after "Shake" should be "High Five." Teach this sequence the same way, but when you hold out your hand to shake,

move your hand up and touch your dog's paw saying, "High five!" It make take a few tries, but by this time your Dachshund will be getting the idea that if he learns his lessons, he gets his treat.

Photo of Stuart from Sheila Paske of Storybook Dachshunds.

This set of four tricks is a good example of using one behavior to build to another. Almost any dog can be taught to perform basic tricks, but don't lose sight of the fact that you are dealing with an individual personality. You may have a Dachshund that would rather chase his chew toys than learn "routines." Get to know what your dog enjoys doing and follow his lead to build his unique set of tricks.

Roll Over

You will find that just like your Dachshund is naturally either right or left pawed, that they will also naturally want to roll to either the right or the left side.

Take advantage of this by asking your dog to roll to the side they naturally prefer. Sit with your dog on the floor and put them in a lie down position.

Hold a treat in your hand and place it close to their nose without allowing them to grab it, and while they are in the lying position, move the treat to the right or left side of their head so that they have to roll over to get to it.

You will quickly see which side they want to naturally roll to; once you see this, move the treat to that side. Once they roll over to that side, immediately give them the treat and praise them.

You can say the verbal cue "Over" while you demonstrate the hand signal motion (moving your right hand in a half circular motion) from one side of their head to the other.

Sit Pretty

While this trick is a little more complicated, and most dogs pick up on it very quickly, remember that this trick requires balance, and every dog is different, so always exercise patience.

Find a quiet space with few distractions and sit or stand in front of your dog and ask them to "Sit."

Have a treat nearby (on a countertop or table) and when they sit, use both of your hands to lift up their front paws into the sitting pretty position, while saying the command "Sit Pretty." Help them balance in this position while you praise them and give them the treat.

Once your Dachshund can do the balancing part of the trick quite easily without your help, sit or stand in front of your dog while asking them to "Sit Pretty" and hold the treat above their head, at the level their nose would be when they sit pretty.

If they attempt to stand on their back legs to get the treat, you may be holding the treat too high, which will encourage them to stand up on their back legs to reach it. Go back to the first step and put them back into the "Sit" position, and again lift their paws while their backside remains on the floor.

The hand signal for "Sit Pretty" is a straight arm held over your dog's head with a closed fist. Place your Dachshund beside a wall when first teaching this trick so that they can use the wall to help their balance.

A young Dachshund puppy should be able to easily learn these basic tricks before they are six months old, and when you are patient and make your training sessions short and fun for your dog, they will be eager to learn more.

Excessive Jumping

Allowing any dog to jump up on a person is a serious mistake, but is a health risk for Dachshunds, placing too much pressure and twisting force on their elongated spines. Beyond this fact, dogs that jump are simply obnoxious. They knock things and people over with their exuberance and cause damaging by scratching.

Fortunately the Dachshund jumps no more than other breeds.
Jumping is one of the most undesirable of all traits in a dog, especially if the animal has muddy paws or is meeting a frail person. Many people are afraid of dogs, and find spontaneous jumping threatening.

Don't make the mistake of assuming that excessive jumping is an expression of friendliness. All too often it's a case of a dominant dog asserting his authority and saying, "I don't respect you."

Dogs that know their proper place in the "pack" don't jump on more dominant dogs. A jumper sees himself as the "top dog" in all situations.

As the dog's master, you must enforce the "no jumping" rule. Anything else will only confuse your pet. Dogs have a keen perception of space. Rather than retreating from a jumping dog, step sideways and forward, taking back your space that he is trying to claim.

You are not trying to knock your dog down, but he may careen into you and fall anyway. Again, always keep in mind the potential for damage to the Dachshund's spinal cord and exercise appropriate judgment. Remain casual and calm. Take slow, deliberate motions and protect the "bubble" around your body. Your dog won't be expecting this action from you, and won't enjoy it.

After several failed jumps, the dog will lose interest when his dominant message is no longer getting across.

Vicki Spencer of Lorindol Standard Smooths: "It is important to praise him when he does have all four feet on the ground. Rewarding good behavior is often forgotten."

Barking Behavior

Of course your Dachshund will bark, but there is a point where it can become excessive barking creating serious problems, especially if you live near other people. Barking is a common issue with Dachshunds. They have a capacity for barking for what seems like hours on end.

If you are in an apartment complex with shared walls, a barking dog can get you thrown out of your home. To get to the bottom of problem barking, you must first try to figure out what is setting your dog off.

Your Dachshund may bark for the following reasons:

Boredom — Being left alone for long periods causes sadness.

Fear — They may sense a threat such as another animal.

Greeting — They love to greet visitors, or perhaps on a walk they want to communicate with another dog. This would usually be accompanied with a wagging tail and maybe jumping up.

Getting Attention — He may need to go outside to go to the toilet, or maybe he wants attention from you or food.

So what can you do when you have an issue?

1. Nip it in the bud by dealing with barking problems as quickly as possible before it escalates.

2. Fence your garden or yard with solid fencing so he feels safer and less threatened.

3. Ignore your Dachshund until he stops barking. You don't want him thinking he can just bark and get what he wants, or he will only keep repeating the behavior.

4. If he barks while you're out and the neighbors complain, he is bored. Don't leave him as long; get someone to come in and play with him or leave toys that occupy him.

5. As with all problem behaviors, address barking with patience and consistency. Don't shout and get angry — he will bark even louder!

6. You can feed him a treat AFTER as a reward but never when he is barking, otherwise he will start to bark to get a treat!

7. For real problem barkers, humane bark collars can teach the dog through negative reinforcement. These collars release a harmless spray of citronella into the dog's nose in response to vibrations in the throat. The system, though somewhat expensive at $100/£60, works in almost all cases.

Lori Darling of Red Oak Dachshunds recommends you start setting ground rules from an early age: "If starting from a puppy the first word I teach them is NO. Just like a young child they will always test you to see what they can get away with. Ignore them to a certain extent depending on the type of barking. If more discipline is required you can also wrap your hand around the dog's muzzle. Do not squeeze, just wrap and in a firm voice tell them NO or

ENOUGH - be firm. The key is to do it every day every time. If dealing with an adult dog, I recommend you get a trainer that deals with behavior issues and will come to your home."

Chewing

Chewing is a natural behavior in dogs and one that Dachshunds take to the extreme. If left undirected, the dogs are capable of causing unbelievable levels of destruction in your home.

Normal chewing relieves anxiety, keeps their jaws strong and their teeth clean. However, excessive chewing indicates some  combination of anxiety or boredom, which may mean you need to get your dog out of the house more. Make sure you are giving your Dachshund plenty of physical and mental stimulation by taking him to the dog park, playing games such as fetch, or enrolling him in activities such as agility.

Puppies go through a teething stage like human babies where they lose their baby teeth and experience pain as their adult teeth grow through. This should be done with by about six months, but before then you can still channel your puppy's urge to chew in the right direction.

Make sure your dog has proper chew toys that exist to be destroyed! Keep things interesting by buying new ones every so often.

Yes, you can give him a bone, but only natural bones that are sold specifically for chewing because cooked bones can splinter and seriously injure him.

If you catch your pet chewing on a forbidden object, reprimand (we don't mean punish) him and take the item away. Immediately substitute an appropriate chew toy and if you chose to, reward him with attention or a treat.

You can buy chewing deterrents such as Grannick's Bitter Apple spray which you spray on all objects that you don't want your dog to chew. Reapply the deterrent every day for two to four weeks.

Digging

Digging indoors, like barking and chewing, can be an expression of fear, anxiety, and/or boredom and is a recognized behavior with Dachshunds. They were, after all, bred to be badger dogs. Their front paws are well adapted for digging down into burrows in pursuit of prey.

Digging is a difficult behavior to stop, especially when it is an instinctual imperative. An out-of-control digger can destroy your sofa or some other piece of furniture. The best solution is to spend more time playing with and exercising your pet and providing your dog with an outdoor sandbox where digging is allowed. Also, consider enrolling your pet in a dog daycare facility so he will not be alone while you are at work and thus less susceptible to separation anxiety.

Begging

Any dog will beg at the table if allowed to do so. My best advice to you is to never allow this behavior to get started. Make "people" food off limits from day one.

If your pet becomes a serious beggar, confine him to another part of the house during meal times. This is as a control measure for you and other people at the table. If you can't ignore a plaintive, begging set of Dachshund eyes, you're the real problem!

Chasing

Dachshunds are excellent runners and trackers. Chasing is another part of their hunting instinct. This can be an enormous danger to your dog if he is not restrained.

When you are out with your dog, especially near busy urban areas, you must keep your pet leashed at all times. Never allow your dog off the leash unless you are in a fenced, completely secure area.

A Dachshund can easily become so intent on the chase, they will not come when called and do not pay attention to dangers in their immediate area, including automobiles.

Biting

Dachshunds can be problem biters, especially when they are stressed or being aggressive over their territory – including you. Try to curb nipping and biting from puppyhood forward and make sure your dog is exposed to a wide range of environments and circumstances.

With their littermates, your Dachshund would have learned about biting. Other puppies would have reacted with fear and noise if they were nipped too hard. This would have curbed the rough play, and this technique can be used when this nipping becomes too painful or dangerous to you.

Make a loud sound and withdraw your attention to imitate the reaction as if from a sibling in the pack. Ignore them each time they bite you too hard until they learn that is the reason.

Any dog will bite if he is reacting out of pain or fear. Biting is a primary means of defense. Use socialization, obedience training, and stern corrections to control a puppy's playful nips.

If an adult dog displays biting behavior, it is imperative to get to the bottom of the biting. Have the dog evaluated for a health problem and work with a professional trainer.

Dealing with Copraphagia

Copraphagia is when dogs eat feces, either their own or that of another animal. While we may be appalled at this, it is actually quite common in dogs. The problem is that nobody really seems to know why this happens. Reasons speculated upon include a lack of nutrition in their diet, being left alone, or learned behavior from their time in the litter.

Mostly they will grow out of this, but how can we discourage it?

1. Clean up after your Dachshund as soon as they have eliminated.

2. Keep him stimulated with chew toys and games and don't leave him alone for long periods.

3. Review his diet — Vitamin-B deficiency is a key suspect, but it could be another nutrient he is lacking.

4. You could feed certain foods that are expelled and smell disgusting to him so he avoids eating them. These include garlic, parsley, and courgettes.

Dachshund Field Trials

Dachshund love to participate in Field Trials and Earth Dog events. Because they are scent hounds, they enjoy using their nose to track game. The American Kennel Club offers these performance events to Dachshunds as well as other breeds.

For the dog, it is exciting and fun. For the owner, it's a thrill to watch the dog work tracking with their nose. It gives owners the opportunity to socialize with other Dachshund owners who enjoy the sport and the breed. Good sportsmanship is always expected in the events.

Field Trials are run mostly in fenced Beagle club grounds where rabbits live. Beagles are another breed that participates in Field Trials of their own.

Photo Credit: Lorraine and Dave Simmons of Stardox Dachshunds - the training photo is one of a standard puppy learning the smell of

rabbit fur. This way it will recognize the scent and track it in a field trial. It's amazing the scenting ability of the Dachshund to track a rabbit in the field by only its footsteps hopping in the field or into the cover of brush without seeing the rabbit.

Dachshunds are braced in twos, and when a rabbit is sighted the person says "Tally Ho." The judges mark a starting spot and take note in their mind where they saw the rabbit go.

The dogs are released when the rabbit is out of sight. The dog who tracks the rabbit scent with the most accuracy as far as the judge saw the rabbit go wins the brace. They are scored and in the end are awarded points towards a Field Championship title. No rabbits are injured during this event. This is strictly tracking the rabbit's foot scent.

Dachshund Earth Dog (Go To Ground)

Dachshunds were badger hunters. Dachshunds participate in the American Kennel Club Earth Dog test. There are three levels of tests that they can compete in. The dogs must complete the requirements of one level before moving on to the next. Each level achieved gives the dog a title.

Level 1. Intro to Quarry. " IQ", Level 2. Junior "JE", Level 3. Senior "SE" and 4. Master " ME". This is a non-competitive sport offered to Dachshunds and small Terrier breeds. Earth Dog measures their natural and trained hunting and working abilities when exposed to a hunting situation. The object is to follow game to ground and work its quarry.

The ground is scented that leads to the tunnel, this being a three-sided wooden liner buried in the ground. Each level has different amounts of turns and length to the quarry. At the end of the earth is the den area, where the caged quarry (two rats) is placed.

The quarry is securely caged and cannot be hurt by the dog, nor can it hurt the dog. An opening at the end allows the judge to observe the dog work and provides a way to remove the dog on completion of the test.

More information can be found on the American Kennel Club website. Field Trials and Earth Dog information kindly written

specifically for this book by **Lorraine and Dave Simmons of Stardox Dachshunds,** who add this final comment: "Dachshunds are a great breed. They can go from sitting on the couch with you to going to an event and enjoying what they were bred to do. Any spayed or neutered dog can participate in AKC performance events such as Earth Dog, Field Trials, Rally, Agility, Obedience, and tracking. Intact dogs may compete in Conformation shows. Dachshunds love to participate in all these events."

Susan Holt of Waldmeister Dachshunds gives a UK perspective: "In the UK, the Kennel Club does not recognise or test the hunting ability of the Dachshund. Therefore owners that are keen to perpetuate the Dachshund's original function, get together for fun tracking days where the dogs follow a pre-laid scent trail — usually there are two tracks laid. A simple track with one or two turns for novices and a more difficult track with several turns and a break in the scent for the more experienced – these days are very popular and give Dachshund owners that chance to socialise."

Chapter 9 – Dachshund Health

This chapter is intended to give owners an indication of some of the common illnesses that may affect their Dachshund. For legal reasons, I have to put in the disclaimer that I am not a qualified veterinarian, and if you have any concerns regarding the health of your dog, you should immediately consult a veterinarian.

You are your Dachshund's primary healthcare provider. You will know what is "normal" for your dog. Yours will be the best sense that something is "wrong" even when there is no obvious injury or illness. The more you understand preventive health care, the better you will care for your dog throughout his life.

First Visit to the Vet

Working with a qualified veterinarian is critical to long-term and comprehensive healthcare. If you do not already have a vet, ask

your breeder for a recommendation. If you purchased your pet outside your area, contact your local dog club and ask for referrals.

Make an appointment to tour the clinic and meet the vet. Be clear about the purpose of your visit and about your intent to pay the regular office fee. Don't expect to get a freebie interview, and don't waste anyone's time! Go in with a set of prepared questions. Be sure to cover the following points:

- How long has this practice been in operation?
- How many vets are on staff?
- Are any of your doctors specialists?
- If not, to which doctors do you refer patients?
- What are your regular business hours?
- Do you recommend a specific emergency clinic?
- Do you have emergency hours?
- What specific medical services do you offer?
- Do you offer grooming services?
- May I have an estimated schedule of fees?

- Do you currently treat any Dachshunds?

Pay attention to all aspects of your visit, including how the facilities appear, and the demeanor of the staff. Things to look for include:

- How the staff interacts with clients
- The degree of organization or lack thereof
- Indications of engagement with the clientele (office bulletin board, cards and photos displayed, etc.)
- Quality of all visible equipment
- Cleanliness of the waiting area and back rooms
- Prominent display of doctors' credentials

These are only some suggestions. Go with your "gut." If the clinic and staff seems to "feel" right to you, trust your instincts. If not, no matter how well appointed the practice may appear to be, visit more clinics before making a decision.

When you are comfortable with a vet practice, schedule a second visit to include your Dachshund puppy. Bring all the dog's medical records. Be ready to discuss completing vaccinations and having the animal spayed or neutered.

Routine exam procedures include temperature and a check of heart and lung function with a stethoscope. The vet will weigh and measure the puppy. These baseline numbers will help chart growth and physical progress. If you have specific questions, prepare them in advance.

Spaying and Neutering

Most reputable purebred Dachshund sales are conducted by way of spay/neuter contracts which stipulate that spaying or neutering is to be completed after the puppy has reached sexual maturity.

Females can get pregnant in old age — they don't go through a menopause. Spaying is the removal of her ovaries and womb (uterus).

Neutering is the removal of the male's testicles, also known as castration, in what is a routine operation. Yes, of course he will feel tender and slightly sore, but this will last only a few days.

Ask yourself, why wouldn't you have these procedures done unless of course you are planning to breed? Don't be swayed by popular misconceptions (myths) such as the operation will subdue or permanently affect his character and personality, or that the dog will gain weight. Remember that dogs are not humans; their need for sex is purely physical, caused by hormones that when removed will mean your dog does not desire or miss sex.

It is very important that spay/neuter procedures are done **after sexual maturity** because there is ongoing emotional maturing that needs to take place. This maturation happens during the final phase of puppy adolescence (usually 9 months to 12 months old) and helps to achieve healthy, balanced adult Dachshund behavior. Sexual maturity happens after a first menstrual cycle, often referred to as being "in heat" or "in season," and takes place in the bitch puppy and after the male dog is capable of having the ability to sire pups.

A female Dachshund will have her menstrual cycle every 6/8 months on average, and this lasts usually 12-21 days. Her hormones will be raging, and through a sense of smell hundreds of times more powerful than ours, the male dogs from miles around will be on alert. You will notice some bleeding (spotting). This is perfectly normal.

Spay and neuter procedures may also carry some health and behavioral benefits:

1. Neutering reduces the risk of prostatic disease or perianal tumors in male dogs.

2. The surgery may also lessen aggressive behaviors, territorial urine marking, and inappropriate mounting.

3. Spayed females have a diminished risk for breast cancer and

no prospect of uterine or ovarian cancer.

4. There is no possibility of an unplanned or unwanted litter.

5. There are no mood swings related to hormones or issues (such as mess) around the bitch coming into season.

6. No unintentional litters from females being bred.

Thanks to **Sheila DeLashmutt of ZaDox Dachshunds** for her advice on this section.

Vicki Spencer of Lorindol Standard Smooths: "New research from some of our top Veterinarian Teaching Universities have shown spay and neutering (especially at a young age) is detrimental to the health of our dogs. Because of this I have changed my contract to state IF spaying/neutering is necessary, the new owner agrees to wait until their puppy is two years old before castrating."

Ian Seath, Chairman of the UK Dachshund Breed Council agrees: "There is a growing body of evidence that this has negative health consequences. Our UK Survey in 2015 showed that neutered dogs/bitches were twice as likely to have IVDD problems."

Photo Credit: Jill Wagner on behalf of Pramada Kennels

Vaccinations

If your Dachshund puppy is not immunized, then he is at risk from potentially fatal canine diseases because he has no protection. Contact with other dogs could occur at parks or at the vets, so be very careful until he has received his first vaccinations. After birth, puppies receive immunity to many diseases from their mother's milk (this is called colostrums), but as they mature, this immunity fades.

Without immunization, your pup won't be covered under any pet insurance policy you may have taken out.

To give a balanced view, I will also point out that some breeders believe some Dachshunds are "over-vaccinated" and while very rare, there is the possibility of a reaction to the vaccine too.

A minor reaction could affect your Dachshund in ways such as, they are sleepy, sneezing, irritable, and they are especially sore or have a lump where injected. These should resolve in a few days.

A more severe reaction requiring immediate treatment would include vomiting, diarrhea, seizures, and a hypersensitivity reaction similar to that of a human anaphylactic reaction.

So what are the worst threats? There are two deadly threats that are the main focus of the initial vaccinations — distemper and parvo virus.

Distemper causes flu-like symptoms initially and progresses to severe painful neurological symptoms such as seizures and often ends in death. The virus is airborne so can be caught if your puppy comes into close proximity to an infected dog.

Parvo virus causes diarrhea and vomiting, often ending in death. The virus can be present in grass or on other surfaces for years.

A puppy's recommended vaccinations begin at 6-7 weeks of age. The most common combination vaccine given is known as **DHPP**.

The initials refer to the diseases included in the vaccine – Distemper, Hepatitis, Parvo, and Parainfluenza. Some vets may also include protection against Coronavirus and the bacteria Leptospirosis at the same time. The first injection thereby protects him from a number of diseases in one go.

In the UK, this first vaccinations tends to include: Distemper, Canine Parvovirus (Parvo), Infectious Canine Hepatitis (Adenovirus), Leptospirosis, and Kennel Cough (Bordetella).

Why the differences? Canine Coronavirus is a relatively new vaccine and so is not offered as standard in every veterinary practice in the UK. Rabies is considered to have been eliminated within the UK, however, if you plan to take your dog out of the country, you will require a pet passport and then they must be vaccinated against rabies.

Recommended boosters occur at 9, 12, and 16 weeks. In some geographical regions in the USA, a vaccine for Lyme disease (typically in forested areas) starts at 16 weeks with a booster at 18 weeks.

The rabies vaccination is administered at 12-16 weeks and yearly for life thereafter, although many states allow 3 years between rabies vaccinations.

Most vaccinations are administered by means of an injection, although kennel cough is usually by a nasal spray.

Once this initial schedule has been completed, the debate opens up over the frequency of boosters. General practice is to give a distemper/parvo booster a year after the completion of their puppy series. After that, it depends on the individual vet, but usually a booster takes place every 3 years after the completion of the initial puppy series.

Once your puppy has had their second set of vaccines, they should be safe to go into the outside world and play with other dogs.

Some of our breeders are in favor of a titer test. This is a straightforward blood test that measures a dog's antibodies to vaccine viruses. Titers accurately assess protection to the core diseases in dogs, enabling veterinarians to judge whether a booster vaccination is really necessary.

Ian Seath, Chairman of the UK Dachshund Breed Council: "On vaccinations, I would suggest people need to speak with their vets about local requirements, but be mindful of the latest WSAVA advice which has moved away from 'annual boosters' for everything."

WSAVA stands for The World Small Animal Veterinary Association. Its membership is made up of global veterinary organizations:

http://www.wsava.org/

Anne Schmidt of Stardust Dachshunds: "Doxies are prone to vaccine reactions, especially LEPTO. It is very important to watch your puppy for 12 hours after vaccines. Also do not give more than one vaccine per vet visit. For example, don't give rabies and DHPP the same day, wait 4 weeks."

Evaluating for Worms

Puppies purchased from a breeder are almost always parasite free because puppies are given their first dose of worming medication at

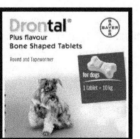

around two weeks old, then again at five and eight weeks before they leave the litter. This is another reason to make sure you buy from a reputable breeder and not someone who doesn't know what they are doing. Worms are more common in rescue dogs, strays, and from "backyard breeders."

I have talked about taking your Dachshund to the vet within days of your purchase to get him health checked. A worm test is usually done then. These tests are important because some parasites, like tapeworms, may be life threatening. Your vet will need a fecal sample for this purpose.

The main types of worms affecting puppies are **roundworm** and **tapeworm**. Roundworms appear as small white granules around the anus. Other types of worms can only be seen through a microscope.

If the puppy tests positive, the standard treatment is a deworming agent with a follow-up dose in 10 days. Most vets recommend worming a puppy once a month until he is six months old, and then around every two or three months.

Dangers to you: Roundworm can pass from a puppy to humans, in the most severe cases causing blindness or miscarriage in women. Make sure you wash your hands immediately after handling your puppy.

Heartworms

Mosquitoes spread heartworms (*Dirofilaria Immitis*) through their bites. They are thin, long parasites that infest the muscles of the heart, where they block blood vessels and cause bleeding. Their presence can lead to heart failure and death. Coughing and fainting, as well as an intolerance to exercise, are all symptoms of heartworm. Discuss heartworm prevention with your vet and decide on the best course of action to keep your pet safe.

Warning Signs of Illness in Your Dachshund

- excessive and unexplained drooling
- excessive consumption of water and increased urination
- changes in appetite leading to weight gain or loss
- marked change in levels of activity
- disinterest in favorite activities
- stiffness and difficulty standing or climbing stairs
- sleeping more than normal
- shaking of the head
- any sores, lumps, or growths
- dry, red, or cloudy eyes

Often the signs of serious illness are subtle. Trust your instincts. If you think something is wrong, do not hesitate to consult with your vet.

"Normal" Health Issues

Although Dachshunds are vigorous, healthy dogs, all canines can face medical issues. The following are "normal" health-related matters that may need veterinary evaluation. Pets that are inattentive or lethargic and that are not eating or drinking should be examined. None of these behaviors are normal for a Dachshund.

Diarrhea

Dachshund puppies, like all small dogs, are subject to digestive upsets. Puppies just will get into things they shouldn't, like human food or even the kitchen garbage. Diarrhea from these causes resolves within 24 hours.

During that time, the puppy should have only small portions of dry food and no treats. Give the dog lots of fresh, clean water to guard against dehydration. If the loose, watery stools are still present after 24 hours, take your Dachshund to the vet.

The same period of watchful waiting applies for adult dogs. If episodic diarrhea becomes chronic, take a good look at your pet's diet. Chances are good the dog is getting too much rich, fatty food and needs less fat and protein. Some dogs also do better eating small amounts of food several times a day rather than have 2-3 larger meals.

Allergy testing can identify the causes of some cases of diarrhea. Many small dogs are allergic to chicken and turkey. A change in diet resolves their gastrointestinal upset immediately. Diets based on rabbit or duck are often used for dogs with such intolerances.

Either a bacteria or a virus can cause diarrhea, which accompanies fever and vomiting. Parasites, in particular tapeworms and roundworms, may also be to blame.

Vomiting

Dietary changes or the puppy "getting into something" can also cause vomiting. Again, this should resolve within 24 hours. If the dog tries to vomit but can't bring anything up, vomits blood, or can't keep water down, take your pet to the vet immediately.

Dehydration from vomiting occurs faster than in a case of diarrhea, and can be fatal. It is possible that your dog may need intravenous fluids.

When your dog is vomiting, always have a good look around to identify what, if anything, the dog may have chewed and swallowed. This can be a huge benefit in targeting appropriate treatment.

Photo Credit: Lois and Ralph Baker of Louie's Dachshunds

Other potential culprits include: hookworm, roundworm, pancreatitis, diabetes, thyroid disease, kidney disease, liver disease, or a physical blockage.

Bloat

Any dog can suffer from bloat. The condition is the second most common cause of death in dogs behind cancer.

Some breeds are at higher risk than others. Also known as gastric dilation / volvulus or GDV, bloat cannot be treated with an antibiotic or prevented with a vaccine. In roughly 50% of cases, bloat is fatal.

In severe cases, the stomach twists partially or completely. This causes circulation problems throughout the digestive system. Dogs that do not receive treatment go into cardiac arrest. Even if surgical intervention is attempted, there is no guarantee of success.

Signs of bloat are often mistaken for indications of excess gas. The dog may salivate and attempt to vomit, pace, and whine. Gas reduction products at this stage can be helpful. As the stomach swells, it places pressure on surrounding vital organs, and may burst. All cases of bloat are a *serious* **medical emergency**.

Larger dogs with deep chests and small waists face a greater risk of developing bloat. These include the Great Dane, Weimaraner, Saint Bernard, Irish Setter, and the Standard Poodle. Despite being a smaller-sized dog, the Dachshund is unfortunately also at risk probably because they have deep chests.

Eating habits also factor into the equation. Dogs that eat one large meal per day consisting of dry food are in a high-risk category. Feed three small meals throughout the day instead. This helps to prevent gulping, which leads to ingesting large amounts of air.

If your Dachshund is on a dry food diet, **don't** let him drink lots of water after eating. Doing so causes the dry food in the stomach to expand, leading to discomfort, and a dilution of the digestive juices.

Limit the amount of play and exercise after meals. A slow walk promotes digestion, but a vigorous romp can be dangerous.

Stress also contributes to bloat, especially in anxious or nervous dogs. Changes in routine, confrontations with other dogs, and moving to a new home can all trigger an attack.

Dogs between the ages of 4 and 7 are at an increased risk. Bloat occurs most often between 2 a.m. and 6 a.m., roughly 10 hours after the animal has had his dinner.

Test your dog's dry food by putting a serving in a bowl with water. Leave the material to expand overnight. If the degree of added bulk seems excessive, consider switching to a premium or organic food.

Keep an anti-gas medicine with simethicone on hand. (Consult with your veterinarian on correct dosage.) Consider adding a **probiotic** to your dog's food to reduce gas in the stomach and to improve digestive health.

If a dog experiences bloat once, his risk of a future episode is greater. Keep copies of his medical records at home, and know the location of the nearest emergency vet clinic.

Allergies

Like humans, dogs also suffer from allergies, and Dachshunds seem especially prone to such problems with roughly 1 in 10 being affected at some stage of their life. Food, airborne particles, and materials that touch the skin can all cause negative reactions as well as reactions to flea bites.

Owners tend to notice changes in behavior that suggest discomfort like itching. Common symptoms include chewing or biting of the tail, stomach, or hind legs, or licking of the paws.

In reaction to inhaled substances, the dog will sneeze, cough, or experience watering eyes. Ingested substances may lead to vomiting or diarrhea. Dogs can also suffer from rashes or a case of hives. Your poor Dachshund can be just as miserable as you are during an allergy attack.

If the reaction occurs in the spring or fall, the likely culprit is seasonal pollen or, in the case of hot weather, fleas. Food additives like beef, corn, wheat, soybeans, and dairy products can all cause gastrointestinal upset.

As with any allergy, take away suspect items or try a special diet. Allergy testing offers a definitive diagnosis and pinpoints necessary environmental and dietary changes. The tests are expensive, costing $200+ / £120+.

The vet may recommend medication, or bathing the dog in cool, soothing water. Special diets are also extremely helpful.

For acne-like chin rashes, switch to stainless steel, glass, or ceramic food dishes. Plastic feeding dishes cause this rash, which looks like blackheads surrounded by inflamed skin. Wash the dog's face in clear, cool water and ask the vet for an antibiotic cream to speed the healing process.

Coughing and/or Wheezing

Occasional coughing is not a cause for concern, but if it goes on for more than a week, a vet visit is in order. A cough may indicate:

- kennel cough
- heartworm
- cardiac disease
- bacterial infections
- parasites
- tumors
- or allergies

The upper respiratory condition called "**kennel cough**" presents with dry hacking. It is a form of canine bronchitis caused by warm, overcrowded conditions with poor ventilation. In most cases, kennel cough resolves on its own.

Photo Credit: Laura Ward owner of Bruno and Baci.

Consult with your veterinarian. The doctor may prescribe a cough suppressant or suggest the use of a humidifier to soothe your pet's irritated airways.

When the cause of a cough is unclear, the vet will take a full medical history and order tests, including blood work and X-rays.

Fluid may also be drawn from the lungs for analysis. Among other conditions, the doctor will be attempting to rule out heartworms.

If your dog has a heart murmur they may cough. Get a chest X-ray to see if the heart is enlarged.

Diabetes

Canines can suffer from three types of diabetes: *insipidus, diabetes mellitus,* and gestational diabetes. All point to malfunctioning endocrine glands and are often linked to poor diet. Larger dogs are in a higher risk category.

- In cases of *diabetes insipidus,* low levels of the hormone vasopressin create problems with the regulation of blood glucose, salt, and water.

- *Diabetes mellitus* is more common and dangerous. It is divided into Types I and II. The first develops in young dogs and may be referred to as "juvenile." Type II is more prevalent in adult and older dogs. All cases are treated with insulin.

- Gestational diabetes occurs in pregnant female dogs and requires the same treatment as diabetes mellitus. Obese dogs are at greater risk.

Abnormal insulin levels interfere with blood sugar levels. Dachshunds face a high risk for diabetes, especially if they become obese.

Symptoms of Canine Diabetes

All of the following behaviors are signs that a dog is suffering from canine diabetes:

- excessive water consumption
- excessive and frequent urination
- lethargy / uncharacteristic laziness

- weight gain or loss for no reason

It is possible your pet may display no symptoms whatsoever. Diabetes can be slow to develop, so the effects may not be immediately noticeable. Regular check-ups help to catch this disease, which can be fatal even when you do not realize that anything is wrong.

Managing Diabetes

As part of a diabetes management program, the vet will recommend diet changes, including special food. Your dog may need insulin injections. Although this may sound daunting, your vet will train you to administer the shots. A dog with diabetes can live a full and normal life. Expect regular visits to the vet to check for heart and circulatory problems.

Dental Care

Chewing is a dog's only means of maintaining his teeth. Many of our canine friends develop dental problems early in life because they don't get enough of this activity. Not all dogs are prone to cavities.

Most do suffer from accumulations of plaque and associated gum diseases. Often, severe halitosis (bad breath) is the first sign that something is wrong.

With dental problems, gingivitis develops first and, if unaddressed, progresses to periodontitis. Warning signs of gum disease include:

- a reluctance to finish meals
- extreme bad breath
- swollen and bleeding gums
- irregular gum line
- plaque build-up
- drooling, and/or loose teeth

Dachshunds are prone to developing gum and tooth disease

because their jaws tend to be small and often their teeth are crowded.

The bacterial gum infection periodontitis causes inflammation, gum recession, and possible tooth loss. It requires treatment with antibiotics to prevent a spread of the infection to other parts of the body. Symptoms include:

- pus at the gum line
- loss of appetite
- depression
- irritability
- pawing at the mouth
- trouble chewing
- loose or missing teeth
- gastrointestinal upset

Treatment begins with a professional cleaning. This procedure may also involve root work, descaling, and even extractions.

With Proliferating Gum Disease, the gums overgrow the teeth, causing inflammation and infection. Other symptoms include:

- thickening and lengthening of the gums
- bleeding
- bad breath
- drooling
- loss of appetite

The vet will prescribe antibiotics, and surgery is usually required.

Home Dental Care

There are many products available to help with home dental care for your Dachshund. Some owners opt for water additives that break up tarter and plaque, but in some cases dogs experience stomach upset. Dental sprays and wipes are also an option, but so is gentle gum massage to help break up plaque and tarter.

Most owners incorporate some type of dental chew in their standard care practices. Greenies Dental Chews for Dogs are popular and well tolerated in a digestive sense. An added plus is that dogs usually love them. The treats come in different sizes and

are priced in a range of $7 / £4.21 for 22 "Teeny Greenies" and $25 / £15 for 17 Large Greenies.

Brushing your pet's teeth is the ultimate defense for oral health. This involves the use of both a canine-specific toothbrush and toothpaste. Never use human toothpaste, which contains fluoride toxic to your dog. Some dog toothbrushes resemble smaller versions of our own, but I like the models that just fit over your fingertip. I think they offer greater control and stability.

The real trick to brushing your pet's teeth is getting the dog comfortable with having your hands in his mouth. Start by just massaging the dog's face, and then progressing to the gums before using the toothbrush. In the beginning, you can even just smear the toothpaste on the teeth with your fingertip.

Try to schedule these brushing sessions for when the dog is a little tired, perhaps after a long walk. Don't apply pressure, which can stress the dog. Just move in small circular motions and stop when the Dachshund has had enough of the whole business. If you don't feel you've done enough, stop. A second session is better than forcing your dog to do something he doesn't like and creating a negative association in his mind.

Even if you do practice a full home dental care routine, don't scrimp on annual oral exams in the vet's office. Exams not only help to keep the teeth and gums healthy, but also to check for the presence of possible cancerous growths.

Anne Schmidt of Stardust Dachshunds: "If your dog will not let you brush their teeth, allow them to chew on knuckle bones, Bull Pizzles, cow ears or trachea. These all help remove tartar and stimulate the gums."

The Matter of Genetic Abnormalities

There are a number of genetic abnormalities and conditions common to Dachshunds. Before you panic, you should realize that every breed has certain ailments that they are more prone to than other breeds.

With the Dachshund, many are associated with the dogs' stubby legs and elongated build. For instance, Dachshunds are said to be chondrodystrophoid. They exhibit abnormal cartilage development, which causes their skeletons to be similar to those of humans with dwarfism. This explains their short legs, which are held up by bones with enlarged ends and pronounced curvature of the bone shaft.

The following are the most common genetic abnormalities present in the breed.

Intervertebral Disk Disease

Intervertebral disk disease (IVD or IVDD) affects more Dachshunds than all other breeds combined. It's the genetics of short legs that pre-dispose Dachshunds to back disease.

All dogs' discs degenerate with age; they lose water, become more fibrous, and sometimes mineralised. Degeneration of a Dachshund's discs happens at a much younger age than in dogs with normal length legs. The condition presents with herniated disks in the lower back causing severe pain that may radiate up to the neck.

Depending on the extent of the issue, surgery may be required, with some Dachshunds experiencing rear-quarter paralysis and the need for medical assistance carts to remain mobile. These devices, which attach to the hips, put your pooch on wheels. Dachshunds adapt well under such circumstances. So long as your pet is otherwise healthy, this is a reasonable approach to a debilitating, but not fatal ailment.

Often called "dog wheelchairs," you can buy these units online from sites like http://www.handicappedpets.com.

Although the carts are adjustable, having your dog custom fitted for the appliance may provide more mobility.

To help guard against instances of IVD, Dachshund owners should not allow their dogs to engage in activities that unduly strain their backs and spines, including excessive jumping or actions that require sudden twisting.

In the first instance, don't buy a puppy from parents with an exaggerated length of body or excessively short legs as these are risk factors for IVD.

You should also keep your Dachshund well-exercised, fed a balanced diet, and at an ideal body condition (not too lean and not overweight). Allow your Dachshund to mature fully before considering neutering.

The main warning signs to watch for include pain (arching of the back, yelping unprovoked), incoordination such as stumbling and swaying, and paralysis.

Photo Credit: Mandy Dance of Emem Dachshunds

Cage rest (typically over 6-8 weeks) combined with anti-inflammatory medication and painkillers are the main conservative treatment approaches likely to be recommended by your vet, where surgery is not felt to be necessary.

Many, if not most, dogs who have surgery within 24 hours of becoming paralysed have more rapid and complete recoveries than dogs who have surgery at a later time. If a dog is paralysed, but still has deep pain sensations, surgery can often result in a complete recovery or a reasonably good recovery with minor neurological deficits.

Further info:

http://www.dachshund-ivdd.uk/
http://www.dodgerslist.com/index.htm

Luxating Patella

A dog with a luxating patella experiences frequent dislocations of the kneecap. The condition is common in small and miniature breeds, and can affect one or both kneecaps. Mini Dachshunds are more prone than standards. Surgery may be required to rectify the problem. Often, owners have no idea anything is wrong with their dog's knee joint. Then the pet jumps off a bed or leaps to catch a toy, lands badly, and begins to limp and favor the leg.

The condition may be genetic in origin, so it is important to ask a breeder if the problem has surfaced in the line of dogs he cultivates. A luxating patella can also be the consequence of a physical injury, especially as a dog ages. For this reason, you want to **discourage jumping** in older dogs. Offer steps in key locations around the home to help your senior Dachshund navigate in safety.

Any time you see your dog limping or seeming more fatigued than usual after vigorous play, have the dog checked out. Conditions like a luxating patella only get worse with time and wear, and need immediate treatment.

Heart Issues

Heart murmurs are an abnormality in the way the heartbeat sounds when listened to with a stethoscope due to an unusual blood flow through the heart. **Wires** are known to be more likely to have this condition than smooth or longhaired Dachshunds.

Many Dachshunds lead perfectly normal lives with this abnormality, but a heart murmur can also be an early sign of a leaking mitral valve. **Mitral valve disease** is the abnormal leaking of blood through the mitral valve, from the left ventricle into the left atrium of the heart. Over time this leak gets worse, eventually resulting in congestive heart failure.

With heart murmurs, although expensive, a cardiac ultrasound exam is recommended to establish the extent of a possible problem. It is also worth asking your breeder whether there has been any history of heart disease in the puppy's pedigree.

Hemangiosarcoma

This is a highly aggressive malignant cancer that arises from the blood vessels, which then rapidly circulates through the bloodstream. Tumors then develop in areas such as the spleen

(around 50%), and also the heart, liver, skin, kidneys, mouth, muscle, bone, brain, and bladder.

Photo Credit: Avril Osborne of Dachshund Dawgz

Hemangiosarcoma is called "The Silent Killer" because signs are usually not apparent until it has metastasized and the tumor has ruptured before treatment is possible. For example, it doesn't show up in blood tests until hemorrhaging has occurred, and ultrasounds fail to detect fast-growing tumors. Unfortunately, at this time the causes are unknown, but a lot of research is being done to understand the disease.

Though Dachshunds are not among the breeds considered at high risk, there are estimated to be around 100 affected each year, mostly in those that are older than 6 years of age.

Warning signs you can look out for include:

- Lethargic and cold
- Lack of appetite
- Wanting to spend time on his own

- Pale gums
- Expanded, fluid-filled abdomen (occurs with tumors in the spleen)

Treatment is by surgery and chemotherapy, although in most cases this does not provide a cure, but it does prolong your dog's life by around six months.

Hip Dysplasia

Dachshunds may also be susceptible to hip dysplasia. This defect prevents the thighbone from fitting into the hip joint. It is a painful condition that causes limping in the hindquarters. Again, this may be inherited, or the consequence of injury and aging. Limit steps until growth plates are closed at 9-12 months.

When hip dysplasia presents, the standard treatment is anti-inflammatory medication. Some cases need surgery and even a full hip replacement. Surgical intervention for this defect carries a high success rate, allowing your dog to live a **full and happy life**.

Canine Arthritis

Dogs, like humans, can suffer from arthritis. This debilitating degeneration of the joints often affects larger breeds, but due to the prevalence of back and joint problems in Dachshunds, arthritis is often seen with the breed.

As the cartilage in the joints breaks down, the action of bone rubbing on bone creates considerable pain. In turn, the animal's range of motion becomes restricted.

Standard treatments do not differ from those used for humans. Aspirin addresses pain and inflammation, while supplements like glucosamine work on improving joint health. Environmental aids, like steps and ramps, ease the strain on the affected joints and help pets stay active.

Arthritis is a natural consequence of aging. Management focuses on making your pet comfortable and facilitating ease of motion. Some dogs become so crippled that their humans buy them mobility carts.

Canine Eye Care

Check your dog's eyes on a regular schedule to avoid problems like clogged tear ducts. Also, many dogs suffer from excessive tearing, which can stain the fur around the eyes and down the muzzle.

As a part of good grooming, keep the corners of your pet's eyes and the muzzle free of mucus to prevent bacterial growth. If your dog is prone to mucus accumulation, ask your vet for sterile eyewash or gauze pads. Also consider having the dog tested for environmental allergies.

With longhaired animals, take the precaution of keeping the hair well-trimmed around your pet's eyes. If you do not feel comfortable doing this chore yourself, discuss the problem with your groomer. Shorter hair prevents the transference of bacteria and avoids trauma from scrapes and scratches.

Dogs love to hang their heads out of car windows, but this can result in eye injuries and serious infection from blowing debris. If you don't want to deprive your dog of this simple pleasure, I recommend a product called Doggles. These protective goggles for dogs come in a range of colors and sizes for less than $20 / £12 per pair. The investment in protecting your dog's eyes is well worth it. All my pets have worn the Doggles without complaint.

Conjunctivitis is the **most common** eye infection seen in dogs. It presents with redness around the eyes and a green or yellow discharge. Antibiotics will treat the infection. The dreaded "cone of shame" collar then prevents more injury from scratching during healing.

Entropion

This is a condition in which the dog's eyelid turns inward, irritating the cornea. The issue becomes apparent in puppies with squinting and excessive tearing. In most cases, the condition resolves as the dog ages. In severe instances, a canine ophthalmologist must tack the lids with stitches that will remain in place for a period of days or weeks until the correct "fit" is achieved. During healing, artificial tears are used to prevent drying of the eyes.

Distichiasis

This painful condition is caused by extra eyelashes growing from abnormal follicles on the inner surface or inside edge of the eyelid. In some cases, there is no problem if the hairs are very small, but if they are long and hard enough, they will cause irritation to the cornea. Results include corneal ulcers, chronic eye and eyelid pain, and excessive tearing.

Treatment is relatively straightforward. Both surgery or electrolysis will remove these abnormal hairs permanently by destroying the hair follicles, preventing re-growth.

Cataracts

Aging dogs often develop cataracts, which is a clouding of the lens of the eye leading to blurred vision. The lesion can vary in size and will be visible as a blue gray area. In most cases, the vet will watch, but not treat cataracts. The condition does not affect your pet's life in a severe way. Dogs adapt well to the senses they do have, so diminished vision is not as problematic as it would be for us.

Cherry Eye

The condition called "cherry eye" is an irritation of the third eyelid. It appears as a bright pink protrusion in the corner of the eye. Either injury or a bacterial infection causes cherry eye. It may occur in one or both eyes and requires surgery to effect a permanent cure.

Glaucoma

With glaucoma, increased pressure prevents proper drainage of fluid. Glaucoma may develop on its own, or as a complication of a shifted cataract. Dogs with glaucoma experience partial or total loss of vision within one year of diagnosis.

Symptoms include swelling, excessive tearing, redness, and evident visual limitations. Suspected glaucoma requires immediate medical attention.

PRA or Progressive Retinal Atrophy

Progressive Retinal Atrophy (PRA), a degenerative hereditary disease, presents with a slow progression. The dog will go blind over time, but most adapt to what is happening to them.

Early detection allows for better environmental adaptations. There is no way to prevent or cure PRA. If you suspect your Dachshund has poor peripheral vision, or if the dog is tentative in low light, have your pet's eyes checked.

Are you buying a Miniature Dachshund? Check they have been DNA tested for PRA.

Hemorrhagic Gastroenteritis

Any dog can develop hemorrhagic gastroenteritis (HGE). The

condition has a high mortality rate. Unfortunately, most dog owners have never heard of HGE. If a dog does not receive immediate treatment, the animal may well die.

Symptoms include:

- profuse vomiting
- depression
- bloody diarrhea with a foul odor
- severe low blood volume resulting in fatal shock

The exact cause of HGE is unknown, and it often occurs in otherwise healthy dogs. The average age of onset is 2-4 years. Approximately 15% of dogs that survive an attack will suffer a relapse. There is no definitive list of high-risk breeds. Those with a high incidence rate include:

- Miniature Poodles
- Miniature Schnauzers
- Yorkshire Terriers
- Dachshunds

The instant your dog vomits or passes blood, get your dog to the vet. Tests will rule out viral or bacterial infections, ulcers, parasites, cancer, and poisoning. X-rays and an electrocardiogram are also primary diagnostic tools for HGE.

Hospitalization and aggressive treatment are necessary. The dog will likely need IV fluids and even a blood transfusion. Both steroids and antibiotics prevent infection. If the dog survives, the animal should eat a bland diet for a week or more with only a gradual reintroduction of normal foods. In almost all cases, the dog will eat a special diet for life with the use of a probiotic.

The acute phases of HGE lasts 2-3 days. With quick and aggressive treatment, many dogs recover well. Delayed intervention for any reason means the outlook is not good.

Lafora

Lafora is an inherited late onset myoclonic epilepsy identified in Miniature Wirehaired Dachshunds. It is a recessive genetic mutation. Characteristics of the disease are shuddering, head jerking, sensitivity to light, and some dogs also develop epilepsy.

Sadly, there is not a completely effective treatment at present, however many are improved on anti-epileptic drugs. Over time, with good breeding, this abnormal gene can be bred out of the Dachshund. There is a DNA test available via a laboratory in Canada and in the UK testing takes place twice yearly organized via Susan Holt (Susan.Holt@talktalk.net) or Nora Price (pn.price274@btinternet.com). Blood is taken in the UK and sent in bulk batches to the Canadian laboratory.

To date, the results of each testing confirm the incidence as 10% affected, 40% carrier, and 50% clear. If a dog has tested positive (affected), this means both parents and all the offspring are either carriers or affected.

Purchasers of puppies should ask breeders the Lafora status of both parents in order not to buy a puppy who might develop the disease. In the UK, all test results are logged on the Kennel Club database and hereditary clear animals are also logged.

Thank you to both Susan Holt and Nora Price for kindly writing this Lafora section to help readers.

Urolithiasis

This condition causes urinary calculi, more commonly known as bladder stones. These are an accumulation of minerals that over time have turned into crystals and stones in a dog's urinary tract.

Obvious signs are frequent urinating and accidents in the home. You may also notice him straining and showing signs of pain.

Bladder stones are caused by bladder infections or are simply genetic. You can help by making sure your Dachshund always has a supply of fresh water and making sure he doesn't have to "hold it in" for long periods of time. You will need to seek out veterinary help quickly before it gets serious. These blockages could prevent the passage of urine, meaning toxins in your dog's waste become trapped in his body. It may be possible to flush out the stones, but otherwise removal by surgery will be necessary.

To prevent recurrence, water consumption should be increased, the pH of the urine measured, and there are dog food manufacturers (e.g., Royal Canin, Purina) that have developed specific diets for dogs with urinary stones.

Breeding Dachshunds

The decision to breed a dog like the Dachshund should only be undertaken for one reason — a desire to improve existing bloodlines mixed with a healthy love for these exceptional animals.

Photo Credit: Nora and Paul Price of Samlane Dachshunds

Breeding pedigreed dogs is not a get-rich quick scheme, nor is it an inexpensive hobby. Before you even contemplate making such a commitment to living creatures, you must be an expert not only in living with and training Dachshunds, but also in reliably pairing animals for the best genetic results.

The purpose of this book is not to educate potential breeders, but to introduce the Dachshund to potential owners. You have a great deal to learn before you can even consider becoming a breeder, but if that is your ultimate goal, start making friends in the Dachshund world now. Cultivating a mentor is an essential step toward owning and operating a successful, well-run breeding operation. Essentially our advice is **to forget it and leave it to the experts!**

Chapter 10 – Interested in Showing Your Dachshund?

If you have purchased a show-quality Dachshund and are planning to enter the world of dog shows and the dog fancy, you have a whole education in front of you.

If you have not already done so, you will want to begin to attend dog shows and to make connections in the world of the dog fancy to acquire the training to participate with your Dachshund, or to hire someone to show the animal for you.

The best thing you can do if you are planning to show your puppy is socializing them once they have settled in their new home. The

work you put in at this stage of your puppy's life will shape them for life, so you need to get it right, take it slowly, and build it up gently. Remember: they are only babies, and they need to know you are there for them and are in charge of every situation.

Photo Credit: Vicki Spencer (right) of Lorindol Standard Smooths with Asher. Presentation from Lorraine Simmons (left) of Stardox Dachshunds who is an AKC Conformation and Field Trial judge.

Your puppy needs to be happy for a judge to run their hands all over them, so it is very important to get them used to this. When your Dachshund puppy is happy for you to be able to touch them all over, you can get your trusted friends to do the same. Start at the head, look in their ears and eyes, and run your hands all down their back and down their legs.

What Dogs Are Qualified to Participate?

For a dog to participate in a dog show, it must be registered with the governing body for that exhibition. For instance, dogs registered with the American Kennel Club that are 6 months or older on the day of the show are eligible to enter AKC sponsored events. Spayed or neutered dogs are not eligible, nor are dogs with disqualifying faults according to the accepted standard for the breed.

It's generally easier to show a male, as opposed to a female, because females can be hard on their coat and change behavior during their heat cycles.

Joining a Breed Club

When you attend a dog show, find out about joining a breed-specific club in your area. Such groups usually sponsor classes to teach the basics in handling and showing the breed or will have contacts to put you in touch with individual teachers.

Breed club membership is also important to learn the culture of the dog fancy and to meet people in the show world. You will begin by participating in smaller, local shows to learn the ropes before entering an event that will garner points toward sanctioned titles within a governing group's system.

There are also "fun matches" that a new dog owner can participate in open to dogs from 3-6 months of age. Here they can get an idea of how dog show judging takes place. It's also a great training ground for that future show prospect.

The more you know about your breed, its care and maintenance, and the handling of them, the better you will be in the show ring. Study your country's parent kennel club's official breed standard.

Hiring a Professional

It is not uncommon for people who own show quality animals to hire professional handlers to work with the dogs.

If you are interested in going this route, be sure to interview several handlers and to get a full schedule of their rates. Attend a show where they are working with a dog and watch them in action. Ask for references, and contact the people whose names you are given.

Entrusting a handler with the care of your dog is an enormous leap of faith. You want to be certain you have hired someone with whom you are completely comfortable and with whom your dog has an observable rapport.

Don't Be Put Off by Fear

My advice to folks who are interested in starting to show is go to several shows and watch the dogs in the ring. Talk to the folks at the sidelines; most are very happy to talk dogs with you.

Find a successful show person to evaluate the dog you plan to start showing. Although anybody can show a dog, you need to get an objective appraisal of your dog's qualities. To qualify as a show dog, it can't have any disqualifying faults, so it is important you find a mentor who can honestly help you evaluate your dog.

I also advise you to attend conformation classes in your area if possible, and be sure your dog is well socialized. Most local Kennel Clubs offer these classes at very reasonable rates. Presentation and the dog's attitude are also a very important factor. Shy and timid dogs usually don't do well at a dog show.

Don't forget that judges' assignments are to assess the breeding stock quality of the exhibits before them via the official breed standard description, observations on movement, and their hands-on experience. There are good judges and the opposite. Many owners have found that performance events, such as obedience, agility, rally, and therapy dog provide great satisfaction in lieu of conformation events.

Of course, you always hope your dog will win. If you have done all your homework, and your dog is a good representative of the breed, you should walk in the ring with confidence and present your dog as best as possible. There is no such thing as a perfect dog, and a good handler will know how to hide the faults and show off the best traits.

I always found going to a dog show exciting. You should always think of it as fun. It will give you an opportunity to meet many people who are also fanciers of your particular breed. Try to learn as much as possible. Hopefully, you will find people who are willing to help.

Although it is a competition, whether you win or lose, you should always be a good sport. Remember, there is always another show and another judge and different competition. After a while, you will get to know which judges like a particular type or style of your breed.

Show Tips and Advice

Make sure you are well organized. Get to the show at least an hour before you are in the ring, as this will give you and your dog time to settle down.

Make sure you have your ring number on when you enter the ring. Make a strong entrance – you only get one chance to make an impression. Remember, the judge will look across the ring from time to time, so have your dog facing the judge even when you are relaxed. Always keep an eye on the judge.

Photo Credit: Sue Ergis of Siouxline Dachshunds

Before you set off, have your arm in an L shape. It will help you keep in a straight line and have more control. Look at something in front of you, keep your eyes on it, and move towards it. Say your dog's name, then say move.

Never give treats when you are moving your dog, as your dog will look up at you, and you need them to go in a straight line. In addition, don't give treats when the judge is going over your dog. Save the treat your dog loves the most for shows, not training, so you can get their attention even more so.

Don't get boxed in a corner at the show; give yourself plenty of room by not standing too close to other exhibiters.

Always dress smart, wear good shoes you can run in, and if you're a woman, wear a sports bra.

Hold your head up, try to look confident, and look like a winner. The judge needs to know you can hold your own and show your dog off in the big ring. If you look too shy, they may think you are not up to the job of representing your breed in the group ring.

Always have a cloth to wipe your dog's mouth dry. Do this just before it's your turn to stand your dog for the judge. It makes showing the bite so much easier.

Warm your dog up before you go in the ring by having a little practice run.

Finally, always take your dog to show in good, clean condition.

Pat Endersby of Mowbray Dachshunds adds: "Start stacking the pup i.e. on a windowsill from 6 weeks old, not for long, but just to get him used to being stood. Also go to a good ringcraft club, so that they learn in a controlled atmosphere."

The Westminster Dog Show and Crufts

So how does an owner get to take part in the famous Westminster Dog Show in the United States?

Maggie Peat of Pramada Kennels knows about this: "It is a requirement that in order to compete, your dog must already have earned a major toward their AKC championship or have an AKC championship. The entry forms are sent out in October of the previous year, and there is a limit to the number of entries that are accepted. This number has increased the last few years and most entries are now accepted if submitted properly within a few days of the first acceptance date in December. You can submit entries online, via USPS or through a third party entry service. In the past, it was more difficult to get your entry received before the limit was reached. Since the class judging moved from Madison Square Garden to the Piers it has become much easier as the limit is higher.

"There is a significant difference between showing at an AKC show and showing at a Kennel Club show. Most AKC shows occur over just ONE day, Westminster being one of the exceptions, and the vast majority of shows are between 500 – 1000 dogs total. There are frequently multiple shows in consecutive days in the same venue, and the chance to win points at each event. If you are just getting started showing in the US, visit a show without entering. Many AKC shows have "Dog Show Tours" or will pair you with an experienced person if you are looking to get started. You can find information on showing at www.akc.org"

Mandy Dance of Emem Dachshunds has been showing for over 30 years and has advice for owners wanting to show at the world-famous Crufts in the UK, as well as some fantastic tips for owners looking to start showing: "Crufts is the only show in the UK where dogs have to qualify to enter by winning at least a 3rd place in their breed at another championship show in the preceding year.

"Despite being another show, Crufts has its own personality unlike any other event. The anticipation and the razzmatazz make it extra special.

"My mini wires will have their preparation started at least two months before the date with a good coat stripping, allowing time for the new coat to be at its best in time for the show. A couple of days before dremelling nails and cleaning teeth takes place together with those all important final coat tweaks.

"Dachshunds are very greedy as we have established and so purchasing the right treats will be important to take. Baked liver pieces or strong cheddar cheese are the favourites in my house.

"Early arrival at Crufts is essential as the mini wires are fired up and ready to go and so need time to adjust to the noise and bustle if they are to concentrate in the ring.

"Handlers make a special effort in their appearance for this particular show and often have to purchase a new jacket for the day! My mini wires show best on a light all in one cord show lead that matches their neck colour as we don't want to break up the neck line.

"Classes are full at this show, with open easily having twenty or more in it.

"The thrill of winning at this prestigious show is quite unlike any other as all eyes are on you. My dogs have had the honour of top wins on many occasions here and these days are remembered forever. I'm convinced the Dachshunds pick up on the vibes of the day as mine always show with extra enthusiasm on the green carpet of Crufts.

"There are plenty of shows apart from Crufts. If you think you might like to exhibit your Dachshund there are different levels of shows that you can go to.

"A good place to start would be with a 'companion show' — dogs don't have to be registered with the Kennel Club and entries are taken on the day. Often in addition to some classes for pedigree dogs, there will be classes for such things as 'best condition,' 'prettiest face' and such like. These are just for fun, but they can be a good place for a novice to practice.

"Following this the next step is a 'limit show.' Here entries are made in advance and it is confined to dogs who have not won major awards.

"The 'open show' is the next level and here any dogs can enter, including champions. Breeds will be scheduled and points can be achieved towards a Junior Warrant.

"The highest level is the 'championship show.' This is where a Cruft's qualification can be won as well as the all important Challenge Certificate. To be a champion, a dog needs to win three challenge certificates under three separate judges in order to achieve their title. All the males in the breed compete in their classes and then all the winners compete against each other to win the dog cc. The same thing happens with all the bitches and then the bitch cc is awarded. The best dog and the best bitch compete against each other to produce the 'best of breed.'

Photo Credit: Anne Schmidt of Stardust Dachshunds

"More information can be found on the Kennel Club website including addresses of local clubs who can help in training for shows: http://www.thekennelclub.org.uk/

"The Dachshund Club website also has useful information and don't forget to ask your dogs' breeder to help you get started."

Chapter 11 – Dachshunds and Aging

It can be heartbreaking to watch your beloved Dachshund grow older – he may develop health problems like arthritis, and he simply might not be as active as he once was. You are likely to notice a combination of both physical and mental (behavior) changes as both body and mind start to slow.

Unfortunately, aging is a natural part of life that cannot be avoided. All you can do is learn how to provide for your Dachshund's needs as he ages so you can keep him with you for as long as possible.

Photo Credit: Dianne Graham of Diagram Dachshunds - this is Dual Champion Diagram Goblet of Fire MW at age 15.

What to Expect

Aging is a natural part of life for both humans and dogs. Sadly, dogs reach the end of their lives sooner than most humans do. Once your Dachshund reaches the age of 11 years or so, he can be considered a "senior" dog.

At this point, you may need to start feeding him a dog food specially formulated for older dogs. Because their **metabolism slows down**, they will put on weight unless their daily calories are reduced. Unfortunately, this weight then places extra stress on their joints and organs, making them work harder than before.

In order to properly care for your Dachshund as he ages, you might find it helpful to know what to expect as your Dachshund dog starts to get older:

• Your dog may be **less active** than he was in his youth – he will likely still enjoy walks, but he may not last as long as he once did, and he might take it at a slower pace.

• Your Dachshund's **joints** may start to give him trouble – check for signs of swelling and stiffness, often due to arthritis, and consult your veterinarian with any problems.

• Your Dachshund may **sleep more** than he once did – this is a natural sign of aging, but it can also be a symptom of a health problem, so consult your vet if your dog's sleeping becomes excessive.

• **Organs**, such as heart or liver, may not function as effectively.

• He may have an occasional "accident" inside the house as a result of incontinence. He may also urinate more frequently.

• Brain activity is affected — your Dachshund's **memory**, ability to learn, and awareness will all start to weaken. He may wander round aimlessly or fail to respond to basic commands.

• He may have a greater tendency to **gain weight**, so you will need to carefully monitor his diet to keep him from becoming obese in his old age.

• He may have **trouble walking** or jumping, so keep an eye on your Dachshund if he has difficulty jumping, or if he starts dragging his back feet.

• Your Dachshund's **vision** may deteriorate. Be careful if his eyes appear cloudy. This could be a sign of cataracts and you should see your vet as soon as you notice this.

• You may need to trim your Dachshund's nails more frequently if he doesn't spend as much time outside as he once did when he was younger.

• He may develop halitosis (bad breath), which can be a sign of dental or gum disease. Get this checked out by a vet. Brush his teeth to a regular schedule.

• Your Dachshund will develop gray hair around the face and muzzle – this may be less noticeable in Dachshunds with a lighter coat.

While many of the signs mentioned above are natural side effects of aging, they can also be symptoms of serious health conditions. If your Dachshund develops any of these problems suddenly, consult your veterinarian immediately.

Caring for an Older Dachshund

When your Dachshund gets older, he may require different care than he did when he was younger.

The more you know about what to expect as your Dachshund ages, the better equipped you will be to provide him with the care he needs to remain healthy and mobile.

Here are some tips for caring for your Dachshund as he ages:

• Schedule routine annual visits with your veterinarian to make sure your Dachshund is in good condition.

• Consider switching to a dog food that is specially formulated for senior/mature dogs – a food that is too high in calories may cause your dog to gain weight. Some are labeled as from age 8, others for even older dogs such as 12+. Take it slow when switching to minimize the impact on their digestive system which cannot cope with sudden change.

• Supplement your dog's diet with DHA and EPA fatty acids to help prevent joint stiffness and arthritis.

• Brush your Dachshund's teeth regularly to prevent periodontal diseases, which are fairly common in older dogs. A daily dental stick helps reduce tartar, freshen breath and improve gum health.

• He may be more sensitive to extreme heat and cold, so make sure he has a comfortable place to lie down both inside and outside.

• Continue to exercise your dog on a regular basis – he may not be able to move as quickly, but you still need to keep him active to maintain joint, muscle health and their vital organs such as heart, lungs and joints exercised.

• Provide your Dachshund with **soft bedding** on which to sleep – the hard floor may aggravate his joints and worsen arthritis.

• Use **ramps** to get your dog into the car and onto the bed (if he is allowed), because he may no longer be able to jump.

• Ensure his usual environment is not too noisy as he will need to rest and sleep more to recharge his body. Make sure it is neither too hot nor cold as his body may not regulate his temperature as well as he used to.

• Consider putting down carpet or rugs on hard floors – slippery hardwood or tile flooring can be very problematic for arthritic dogs.

• Keep your Dachshund's **mind exercised** as well as his body. Playing games and introducing new toys will achieve this.

In addition to taking some of the precautions listed above in caring for your elderly Dachshund, you may want to familiarize yourself with some of the health conditions your dog is likely to develop in his old age.

Elderly dogs are also likely to exhibit certain changes in behavior, including:

- Confusion or disorientation
- Increased irritability
- Decreased responsiveness to commands
- Increase in vocalization (barking, whining, etc.)
- Heightened reaction to sound
- Increased aggression or protectiveness
- Changes in sleep habits
- Increase in house soiling accidents

As he ages, these tendencies may increase – he may also become more protective of you around strangers.

As your Dachshund gets older, you may find that he responds to your commands even **less frequently** than he used to.

The most important thing you can do for your senior dog is to schedule regular visits with your veterinarian. You should also, however, keep an eye out for signs of disease as your dog ages.

Photo Credit: Shirley Ray of Raydachs/TheWinningImage.com

The following are common signs of disease in elderly dogs:

- Decreased appetite
- Increased thirst and urination
- Difficulty urinating/constipation
- Blood in the urine
- Difficulty breathing/coughing
- Vomiting or diarrhea
- Poor coat condition

If you notice your elderly Dachshund exhibiting any of these symptoms, you would be wise to seek veterinary care for your dog as soon as possible.

Dianne Graham of Diagram Dachshunds observes: "Senior Dachshunds are those at age 11 and up. They have silver in their faces. They sleep more but when awake are just as keen as they were when they were puppies, but not for as long. With good veterinary care and proper nutrition, they can live for many more years. I don't feed them any differently than when they were young, unless they start getting plump, at which time I cut back on their food. As the years go by, these beloved members of our family slow down more and more but are still are still valued members of our family."

Euthanasia

The hardest decision any pet owner makes is helping a suffering animal to pass easily and humanely. I have been in this position. Even though I know my beloved companions died peacefully and with no pain, my own anguish was considerable. Thankfully, I was in the care of and accepting the advice and counsel of exceptional veterinary professionals.

This is the crucial component in the decision to euthanize an animal. For your own peace of mind, you must know that you have the best medical advice possible. My vet was not only knowledgeable and patient, but she was kind and forthright. I valued those qualities and hope you are as blessed as I was in the same situation.

I am fortunate that I have never been forced to make this decision based on economic necessity. I once witnessed the joy of a biker who sold his beloved motorcycle to pay for cancer treatments for his German Shepherd. The dog meant more to him than the bike, and he burst into tears when the vet said, "We got it all."

But the bottom line is this: No one is in a position to judge you. No one. You must make the best decision that you can for your pet, and for yourself. So long as you are acting from a position of love, respect, and responsibility, whatever you do is "right."

Grieving a Lost Pet

Some humans have difficulty fully recognizing the terrible grief involved in losing a beloved canine friend.

There will be many who **do not understand** the close bond we humans can have with our dogs, which is often unlike any we have with our human counterparts.

Your friends may give you pitying looks and try to cheer you up, but if they have never experienced the loss of such a special connection themselves, they may also secretly think you are making too much fuss over "just a dog."

For some of us humans, the loss of a beloved dog is so painful that we decide never to share our lives with another, because the thought of going through the pain of such a loss is unbearable.

Expect to feel terribly sad, tearful, and yes, depressed, because those who are close to their canine companions will feel their loss no less acutely than the loss of a human friend or life partner.

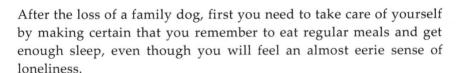

Photo Credit: Connie & Gary Fisher of Beldachs Between the Hills

The grieving process can take some time to recover from, and some of us never totally recover.

After the loss of a family dog, first you need to take care of yourself by making certain that you remember to eat regular meals and get enough sleep, even though you will feel an almost eerie sense of loneliness.

Losing a beloved dog is a shock to the system that can also affect your concentration and your ability to find joy or be interested in participating in other activities that are a normal part of your daily life.

Other dogs, cats, and pets in the home will also be grieving the loss of a companion and may display this by acting depressed, being off their food, or showing little interest in play or games.

Therefore, you need to help guide your other pets through this grieving process by keeping them busy and interested, taking them for extra walks, and finding ways to spend more time with them.

Wait Long Enough

Many people **do not wait long enough** before attempting to replace a lost pet and will immediately go to the local shelter and rescue a deserving dog. While this may help to distract you from your grieving process, this is not really fair to the new fur member of your family.

Bringing a new pet into a home that is depressed and grieving the loss of a long-time canine member may create behavioral problems for the new dog that will be faced with learning all about their new home, while also dealing with the unstable energy of the grieving family.

A better scenario would be to **allow yourself the time to properly grieve** by waiting a minimum of one month to give yourself and your family to feel happier and more stable before deciding upon sharing your home with another dog.

Managing Health Care Costs

Thanks to advances in veterinary science our pets now receive viable and effective treatments. The estimated annual cost for a medium-sized dog, including health care, is $650 / £387. (This does not include emergency care, advanced procedures, or consultations with specialists.)

The growing interest in pet insurance to help defray these costs is understandable. You can buy a policy covering accidents, illness, and hereditary and chronic conditions for $25 / £16.25 per month. Benefit caps and deductibles vary by company.

Although breeders are now becoming more responsible in improving the overall health of a breed, it is inevitable that you will need to make a number of visits to the vets in your Dachshunds lifetime. Apart from the routine of annual injections and check-ups there are bound to be "unexpected" visits often at weekends or in the middle of the night when costs are significantly higher. This total can run to thousands of dollars (or pounds).

Establishing a healthy record from the very beginning ensures your Dachshunds qualifies for full insurance coverage and lower premiums.

Andra O'Connell of Amtekel Longhair Dachshunds agrees: "I believe in preventive maintenance as much as possible. My dogs are seen by a veterinary chiropractor fairly regularly from the time they are about 9 weeks old. My dogs are well exercised to avoid the 'weekend athlete' injuries. We have been blessed with overall sound and healthy Dachshunds."

To get rate quotes, investigate the following companies in the United States and the UK:

United States of America

http://www.24PetWatch.com
http://www.ASPCAPetInsurance.com
http://www.PetsBest.com
http://www.PetInsurance.com

United Kingdom

http://www.Animalfriends.org.uk
http://www.Healthy-pets.co.uk
http://www.Petplan.co.uk

Afterword

In summary, because they are so comical and have such massive personalities, Dachshunds are wrongly perceived as "easy" dogs. They are challenging and at times stubborn, but that is what is so attractive about them!

Without question, if you learn everything there is to know about Dachshunds and believe with all your heart that this is the dog for you, you will never have a better canine companion.

Photo Credit: Lori Darling of Red Oak Dachshunds

Dachshunds are one of the most popular of all breeds for a good reason. They are beautiful creatures with massive amounts of courage and heart. The dogs are devoted, loyal, affectionate, and just plain fun.

I have no doubt that a Dachshund will live up to your every expectation of what a perfect dog should be, just make sure you can be the perfect human for him!

Once again, thank you for purchasing this book. As mentioned in the acknowledgment section, if you would like to receive the free bonus interviews from Dachshund breeders, then go to our webpage here to download your free gift:

http://www.dogexperts.info/dachshund/gift

Bonus Chapter 1 - Dachshunds in the United Kingdom

In this special chapter, Ian Seath, Chairman of the Dachshund Breed Council has kindly agreed to answer some questions in order to help our UK readers understand more about the Dachshund in the United Kingdom.

Ian, perhaps you could start by giving us a bit of background about how the Dachshund came to the UK in the first place?

The origins of the Dachshund can be traced back to working dogs that could go to ground after badgers, foxes and, in the case of Miniatures, rabbits. Germany is usually credited with being the country of origin, but there are numerous references to short-legged working dogs in France, Scandinavia and elsewhere.

There were numerous dogs imported from Germany in the mid to late 19th century and they were present in the Royal kennels as well as several private kennels. The first English book devoted entirely to the breed, "Der Dachshund", was written by Major Emil Ilgner in 1896.

The fact that the UK Dachshund Club was formed in 1881 and predates the Deutscher Teckel Club (1888) is evidence of the breed's popularity.

Today, in the UK, Dachshunds come in two sizes – Standard and Miniature – and three coats – Smooth-haired, Long-haired and Wire-haired. Standards should ideally weigh 20 – 26 lbs and

Miniatures 10 – 11 lbs.

Dachshunds are still used by some people for working; typically tracking fallen deer, and these are often called Teckels. They tend to be slighter in body and longer in the leg than "show" Dachshunds, but are highly regarded for their working ability and "good noses".

Is the Dachshund becoming more or less popular would you say compared to other popular breeds?

Dachshunds are very popular as pets in the UK and make loyal companions. We have seen an enormous rise in registrations of the Miniature Smooth variety, in particular. In 2015 they accounted for just under a quarter of the Hound Group registrations.

This increase in popularity has no doubt been fuelled by their frequent appearance in television and press advertising campaigns. Mini Smooths also have a number of celebrity owners and are seen regularly on programmes. We worry that a combination of today's celebrity culture and "must have one now" attitudes are leading to unsuitable owners buying from unsuitable breeders and importers who are driving up prices.

It's easy to see how the breed has become so popular; they may be small dogs, but they have huge personalities and they are most definitely hounds (with a hint of terrier determination), not lapdogs or toys!

How did you come to own and breed Dachshunds yourself?

My wife and I bought our first Dachshunds, 2 Mini Long dogs, in 1980. We wanted a small dog as we lived in a flat and it seemed that having two would be a good idea as they like being with other Dachshunds as well as with people. Sue started showing them and we discovered and fell in love with the Standard Wires. As soon as we were able to buy a house with a garden we went to one of the most successful UK Wire breeders and bought a Wire bitch. By that time Sue was hooked on showing and the rest, as they say, is history. We bred our first Wire litter in 1984 and the puppy we kept was our first Challenge Certificate winner. We have also owned Mini smooths for the last 10 years, but wires are our first love!

Do Dachshunds in the UK differ greatly from those in the USA?

I don't think there is any great difference between type in US and UK Dachshunds. There may be some slight differences in the way dogs are groomed and presented, but the underlying dogs are similar. Over the years, some UK dogs sent to the US have become established as influential founders of the breed. The reverse is also happening. Since the relaxation of UK quarantine regulations, the UK has seen a number of quality American imports who have had an important impact on the breed. These days, dog breeding and showing is a truly international affair and, I would say, this is

reducing the variation in type that we see.

What official organisations are there for the new Dachshund owner in the UK and what benefits or services do they provide?

The Dachshund Breed Council was set up to be a united voice for the Dachshund Breed in the UK.

It is a Kennel Club registered organisation and, as such, has to comply with the Kennel Club rules and regulations for Breed Councils. There are no individual members of a Breed Council, its members are the 17 Dachshund Breed Clubs.

Anyone owning a Dachshund in the UK is welcome to join one of these clubs. They are a source of advice and expertise which are willingly passed on to new owners. The clubs run a variety of events including shows, seminars and fun days. While shows might be for the more "serious" Dachshund owners, fun days provide an opportunity to participate with like-minded people in activities such as lure racing, mini agility and fun classes like "waggiest tail"!

The clubs also help educate potential new owners at events such as Discover Dogs and various regional pet shows.

In buying a Dachshund, can you offer advice and tips to new owners?

Most puppy buyers use the internet to look for puppies, these days. There's nothing wrong with that, but it's up to you as a buyer to do your research and it can be very confusing because bad breeders will claim many of the same things that good ones do.

We strongly recommend that people ask a Breed Club Secretary for recommendations of breeders before visiting puppies, or committing to buy a puppy. Never buy from a pet shop or "pet supermarket", however "up-market" they appear to be. Their puppies will almost certainly have come from puppy farms or "back-yard breeders", where dogs are bred and reared in poor conditions, purely for profit and with little or no regard for health and welfare.

A reputable breeder will, as a minimum, comply with the good practice requirements of the Kennel Club's Assured Breeder Scheme and will always be happy to answer any queries at any stage of your dog's life. Reputable breeders will want you to be assured that your puppy has been well reared and is a fit, healthy and typical specimen of the breed.

Breeders who are members of a Dachshund Breed Club will comply with our Code of Ethics which covers matters such as health testing, the age at which a bitch should be bred from and the maximum number of litters a bitch should have. Breed Club members will be aware of the relevant health tests which are recommended for Dachshunds and should be able to talk knowledgeably about the relevance of these.

Health is always a major concern when buying a dog, do you have any advice for new Dachshund owners to be aware of in particular?

Dachshunds generally suffer few health problems providing they are kept well exercised and fed a healthy, balanced diet. On average, they live to more than 12 years old.

Because they are a dwarf breed there is an increased risk of back problems (IVDD). Always ask about any history of back problems when buying a puppy and avoid buying puppies from parents with exaggerated length of body or excessively short legs as these are risk factors for IVDD. Problems are best avoided by keeping the dog fit and not allowing it to become overweight, or to run up and down stairs which puts extra stress on the back. We are currently working on the launch of an X-ray screening programme for UK Dachshunds which we hope will help to reduce the prevalence of IVDD.

Mini Long, Mini Smooth and Mini Wire breeding stock should have been DNA tested for Retinal Degeneration (cord1 mutation P.R.A.) which is an inherited condition causing degenerative disease of the retina, resulting in visual impairment, or blindness. Mini Wire breeding stock should have been DNA tested for Lafora Disease (a form of epilepsy).

Always consult a Vet if you have any concerns about a puppy you intend to purchase, or health problems with an older dog.

Breed Club Secretaries will also be able to provide up-to-date advice on any current or emerging health concerns in any of the Dachshund breeds.

If a new owner perhaps wanted to meet other owners or find out more - perhaps they have an interest in joining a local club or maybe they wonder how they can start showing their Dachshund - where would they begin?

A good starting point is the UK Dachshund Breed Council's website http://dachshundbreedcouncil.org.uk/ where people can find contact details of the various national and regional clubs. Talk to one of the Club Secretaries and find out when there's a show you could visit, to meet breeders and owners. Most clubs also have active Facebook pages and there are many local Facebook Groups that organise walks and other get-togethers. Wherever you live in the UK, there will be some Dachshund activity to take part in and knowledgeable people to provide advice.

Bonus Chapter 2 - Choosing and Training Your Puppy

By Karen R. Scheiner of Harlequin Dachshunds

All puppies are cute, especially Dachshund puppies! But choosing a puppy from a litter, with the purpose of deciding which one will be the best one for you and your family, is not puppy's play. If you want to start training a very young puppy, or you are looking to buy a Dachshund puppy for a pet or to enter in performance events, then this chapter is written especially for you.

CHOOSING THE RIGHT PUPPY

All Dachshund puppies are *not* born equal. That is to say, aside from their appearance, some are shy, some are inquisitive, and some are outgoing. The cutest puppy in the litter may be the one that is always hiding in the corner. An inexperienced buyer might easily

fall in love with that shy little puppy in the corner. If you are looking for "just a pet" (translate "couch potato"), then that puppy may be a good fit. However, if you want a playful, outgoing puppy, then the one who seems friendly and fearless is the best one to choose, as it will likely turn out to be sociable and seek interaction with family members.

If you have the opportunity to select a puppy from its litter, bring a squeak toy, something that will rattle or crackle (like a small box with treats, or an empty water bottle), a bouncing ball, or other objects that might create curiosity in a new puppy. Then sit on the floor with all of the puppies and hold your hands out. Observe which ones come running up to you, and which ones hide or seem fearful. Squeak the toy or crackle a bottle, and identify which puppies are afraid of the noise, and which will bravely come to investigate. Shake the can and see if any of the puppies back away, or are any of them running to see what's in it. If you toss a small bouncing ball, which ones give chase? This can give you a good preliminary idea what the puppy will be like as an adult. Choose the puppy with focus and temerity.

FOUNDATION TRAINING

Okay, so now your "star" three-month old puppy is home with you. What next? Foundation training should provide the basic blocks for all other training to be built on. To set the record straight, if you think that immediately enrolling in a puppy training class offered in your area is the right answer, you would be **wrong**. This is a common mistake of new owners. In fact, taking a very young Dachshund puppy to formal training can undermine even your best intentions, for several reasons. First, unless you find a class strictly dedicated to small dogs, you will find a lot of large puppies enrolled in the beginner class that are unruly and unmanageable. They may want to sniff or chase your little puppy, and sometimes the owners cannot even control them! Being chased by a large dog, even in play, can be devastating for a small young puppy. If you are going to go to a puppy class, call first to make sure that there are small breed dogs enrolled. Second, you can (and should) lay the groundwork yourself for the puppy to begin to learn. Finally, and most important, a puppy that is not yet six months old is really too young for formal training classes anyway. Save class time for when your puppy is about a year old, when his attention span will be greater than that of a flea.

To be clear, I am certainly not saying that you should not train a young puppy. Rather, what I *am* saying is that you already have all of the foundation tools you need to work with your puppy at home for at least three to four months. Forget the formal training classes for now.

So let's begin. All foundation training must be fun for the puppy. Fun is the operative word here. Stay upbeat and positive. If you had a bad day at work, it is not the puppy's fault; no yelling at the puppy! Lots of praise, treats and energy go a long way! Try to keep the word, no! out of your vocabulary. You will shut down a puppy with negativity and create unnecessary stress. For example, if the puppy runs away with your favorite sock, force yourself to say, "good boy" in a high positive tone, and then exchange a toy for

your sock. All information in training should be positive with lots of rewards for your puppy. Keep little toys with squeakers or bells in your pockets; have some Cheerios on hand all of the time. PetStages®, AZanies® and Kong®, are just a few of many brands that make a line of interesting small toys designed for puppies.

Socialize your puppy from the beginning. Get your puppy familiar with noises and the environment. Take the puppy for car rides often. Go to the pet store, a pet-friendly mall, and out to the park. Let other people feed him treats and pet him. Take the puppy to your friends' houses (with permission). Let the puppy play with children, especially if none are in your home. Inspire your puppy with treats and toys, to play with you, to walk with you, and to come to you. Get the puppy used to wearing a collar and a four-foot leash. (Stay away from flexi-leads in the beginning; they have their place in training, but not with a young puppy.) Remember that failing to socialize your puppy at an early age can be devastating later, when you want your adult dog to feel comfortable around other people, or even other dogs. Play games with the puppy by having him look at you and then feed a Cheerio as a reward. The importance of these basic initial experiences cannot be overstated enough.

Keep your normal household routine. Run the vacuum, the washing machine, your hair dryer, the television, and any other appliances that are noisy. Let the puppy watch and listen. Remember, when you are in the obedience ring, you don't want your dog to be startled by any noises. Get him used to *everything* from the beginning. These are experiences that cannot be made up later.

Collar and Leash. Put a quick-release collar on your puppy at a very early age and let him get used to wearing it for the first week without anything attached. In about a week, attach a 4-foot leash and try to get him to walk with you. If the puppy won't walk willingly, show him some little treats (like Cheerios or string cheese) in your left hand, and he will follow the treats. This is not to be considered bribing, but rather motivating. A favorite toy will sometimes work here, too, but Dachshunds are famous for being food-motivated. Stay positive and happy. If the puppy takes just a few steps with you, stop and praise. Get excited. Yay!! Good boy!!

Occasionally, turn and face the puppy. With the leash on, say his name and "come!" in an excited manner. Gently reel him in and offer a treat. If the puppy is bucking, you are going too fast. Take it slow. The purpose of these exercises is to get the puppy to happily walk along with a leash and to learn that coming to you is a positive experience. Don't even try formal heeling or recalls until the puppy is comfortable walking on a leash for at least a few months.

Toys and Games. Every "task" should be a non-threatening game for a young puppy. Allow the puppy to carry different objects in his mouth. Put different objects on the floor and see if he will pick them up. If you want the puppy to retrieve items (such as dumbbell or gloves) for you later, then start teaching that skill when he is young.

If you put a few little treats in a tiny Altoids can, the puppy will smell the treats and want to pick it up, and may even bring it to you! This is a great preview for training retrieve of metal object, which are not usually favorites. The puppy should get a treat from the can whenever he picks it up. Gloves or socks are great for chasing and "get it!" When they retrieve it, they earn a treat. All of this is laying foundation for later, more advanced, training skills.

Tug-of-war, or what I call "bouncy bounce" is a great game for interaction. Get a bungie toy — they look like colorful snakes or have balls on either end, with elastic through the middle. The elastic allows the puppy to pull on the toy while you are still holding it. Lightly bounce it up and down while the puppy is on the other end. He will pull harder and love the attention. Some of my doxies love this game so much that (if I let them), they will be bringing the toy to me all day long to pull. This is also great game to play later, with an adult dog, when you are doing warm ups for performance competition, as it can really stimulate them!

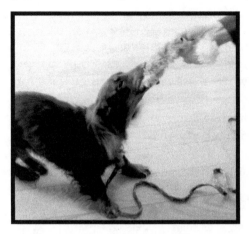

There are certain toys that I never let the dogs take away for individual play, as I always want to be able to pull out a special toy for interaction. In my house, the toy of choice is the stuffingless chipmunk! Made by Skinneeez® and also by Zanies®, you can find stuffing-free squirrels and chipmunks at the pet store or on-line. They have squeakers in the head and tail, and the body is like a flat furry animal. Why do I keep the toy from the dog? So that the dog realizes that to have fun with that toy, it has to come from ME. Your puppy should quickly learn that all good things come from you!

FINAL TIP

One other secret, as a final tip, to keeping your puppy focused on you, the owner. When all else fails, try hand-feeding. That is, instead of just putting the puppy's food dish on the floor, where he can casually feed himself, you intervene as his "helper" so to speak. You can either scoop the food out of the bowl with your hand, or just keep your hands in or near his dish, making him aware of your presence. At least, for the first few weeks that he is with you, you should try this. This will reinforce for him that you are the source of his food and his fun — after all, what else is there in life? Also, a puppy who is used to being hand-fed or seeing your hand in his dish, will never growl or in any way perceive that his food source is being threatened, when he is older.

There should be one person in the house who regularly feeds the puppy and is the primary caretaker. That is the person that the puppy will be most bonded to. Parenthetically, if you have a child who is to be the "owner," then the child should try hand-feeding. Early on, this can create a major difference in how the puppy responds to you and whether he is willing to work for you in the performance ring.

The suggestions in this chapter are intended to serve as a springboard for your own ideas and games as your puppy develops. They are not exclusive, as there are a myriad of ways for socialization, playing games, and getting ready for the performance ring. Just always remember to keep it fun, stay upbeat and positive. Above all, enjoy your new Dachshund puppy!

Karen R. Scheiner of Harlequin Dachshunds

This additional chapter has been especially written for the book by Karen R. Scheiner who is passionate about training Dachshunds. Her achievements include an award for number 2 obedience Dachshund in the country by the National Miniature Dachshund Club. She has also had many others in the top 10 of all Dachshunds in the USA.

Relevant Websites

Dachshund Club of America
www.Dachshundclubofamerica.org

Dachshund Rescue of North America
http://www.drna.org/

National Miniature Dachshund Club
www.Dachshund-nmdc.org

American Kennel Club
http://www.akc.org/

United Kingdom

UK Dachshund Breed Council
http://dachshundbreedcouncil.org.uk/

The UK Dachshund Club
http://www.Dachshundclub.co.uk

British Dachshund Rescue
http://www.dachshundrescue.org.uk/

Miniature Dachshund Club
http://www.miniaturedachshundclub.co.uk/

Smooth-haired Dachshund Club
http://www.smoothhaireddachshundclub.co.uk/

Longhaired Dachshund Club
http://www.thelonghaireddachshundclub.co.uk/

Wirehaired Dachshund Club
http://www.whdc.co.uk/

The Kennel Club
https://www.thekennelclub.org.uk/

Glossary

Abdomen – The surface area of a dog's body lying between the chest and the hindquarters also referred to as the belly.

Allergy – An abnormally sensitive reaction to substances including pollens, foods, or microorganisms. May be present in humans or animals with similar symptoms including, but not limited to, sneezing, itching, and skin rashes.

Anal glands – Glands located on either side of a dog's anus used to mark territory. May become blocked and require treatment by a veterinarian.

Arm – On a dog, the region between the shoulder and the elbow is referred to as the arm or the upper arm.

Back – That portion of a dog's body that extends from the withers (or shoulder) to the croup (approximately the area where the back flows into the tail.)

Bitch – The appropriate term for a female dog.

Blooded – An accepted reference to a pedigreed dog.

Breed – A line or race of dogs selected and cultivated by man from a common gene pool to achieve and maintain a characteristic appearance and function.

Breed standard – A written "picture" of a perfect specimen of a given breed in terms of appearance, movement, and behavior as formulated by a parent organization, for example, the American Kennel Club or in Great Britain, The Kennel Club.

Brows – The contours of the frontal bone that form ridges above a dog's eyes.

Buttocks – The hips or rump of a dog.

Castrate – The process of removing a male dog's testicles.

Chest – That portion of a dog's trunk or body encased by the ribs.

Coat – The hair covering a dog. Most breeds have both an outer coat and an undercoat.

Come into Season – The point at which a female dog becomes fertile for purposes of mating.

Congenital – Any quality, particularly an abnormality, present at birth.

Crate – Any portable container used to house a dog for transport or provided to a dog in the home as a "den."

Crossbred – Dogs are said to be crossbred when each of their parents is of a different breed.

Dam – A term for the female parent.

Dew Claw – The dew claw is an extra claw on the inside of the leg. It is a rudimentary fifth toe.

Euthanize – The act of relieving the suffering of a terminally ill animal by inducing a humane death, typically with an overdose of anesthesia.

Fancier – Any person with an exceptional interest in purebred dogs and the shows where they are exhibited.

Groom – To make a dog's coat neat by brushing, combing, or trimming.

Harness - A cloth or leather strap shaped to fit the shoulders and chest of a dog with a ring at the top for attaching a lead. An alternative to using a collar.

Haunch Bones – Terminology for the hip bones of a dog.

Haw – The membrane inside the corner of a dog's eye known as the third eyelid.

Head – The cranium and muzzle of a dog.

Hip Dysplasia – A condition in dogs due to a malformation of the hip resulting in painful and limited movement of varying degrees.

Hindquarters – The back portion of a dog's body including the pelvis, thighs, hocks, and paws.

Hock – Bones on the hind leg of a dog that form the joint between the second thigh and the metatarsus. Known as the dog's true heel.

Lead – Any strap, cord, or chain used to restrain or lead a dog. Typically attached to a collar or harness. Also called a leash.

Litter – The puppy or puppies from a single birth or "whelping."

Muzzle – That portion of a dog's head lying in front of the eyes and consisting of the nasal bone, nostrils, and jaws.

Neuter – To castrate or spay a dog thus rendering them incapable of reproducing.

Pedigree – The written record of a pedigreed dog's genealogy. Should extend to three or more generations.

Puppy – Any dog of less than 12 months of age.

Separation Anxiety – The anxiety and stress suffered by a dog left alone for any period of time.

Sire – The accepted term for the male parent.

Spay – The surgery to remove a female dog's ovaries to prevent conception.

Whelping – Term for the act of giving birth puppies.

Withers – The highest point of a dog's shoulders.

Index

CPSIA information can be obtained
at www.ICGtesting.com
Printed in the USA
BVHW071024230919
559149BV00009B/482/P